OPPOSING VIEWPOINTS SERIES
Volume Ten

AMERICAN VALUES

OPPOSING VIEWPOINTS

DAVID L. BENDER
Editor

GREENHAVEN PRESS — ANOKA, MINNESOTA 55303

© Copyright 1975 by Greenhaven Press, Inc.

ISBN 0-912616-16-4 Paper Edition
ISBN 0-912616-35-0 Cloth Edition

TABLE OF CONTENTS

INTRODUCTION   1

Chapter I: WHAT DOES AMERICA STAND
           FOR?
   1.   THE AMERICAN CHARACTER   4
        William Fulbright
   2.   THE BIBLE OF AMERICANISM   14
        Daniel L. Marsh

Chapter II: AMERICAN BUSINESS VALUES
   3.   BUSINESS IS THE SOURCE OF OUR   29
        VALUES
        Otto A. Bremer
   4.   THE BUSINESSMAN'S RIGHT TO   36
        PROFIT
        Edward Maher
   5.   THE GOSPEL WAY AND THE   44
        AMERICAN WAY ARE
        CONTRADICTORY
        Eugene C. Bianchi
   6.   COMPETITION IS ESSENTIAL   53
        James M. Roche
   7.   CAPITALISM IS DESTROYING   60
        AMERICA
        Thomas Christoffel
   8.   GOVERNMENT REGULATIONS   70
        ARE DESTROYING CAPITALISM
        Hans F. Sennholz

Chapter III: AMERICAN POLITICAL VALUES
   9.   INDIVIDUAL RESPONSIBILITY   81
        AND FREEDOM
        Dean Russell
  10.   THE NEW ARISTOCRACY   89
        Sidney Lens
  11.   BELIEFS AND PRINCIPLES OF THE   97
        JOHN BIRCH SOCIETY
        John H. Rousselot
  12.   OUR UNSPOKEN NATIONAL   101
        FAITH
        Daniel J. Boorstin

Chapter IV: AMERICAN SOCIAL VALUES
13. COOPERATION INSTEAD OF   113
     COMPETITION
     Ashley Montagu
14. AMERICAN VIRTUES: 117
     INDIVIDUALISM AND
     SELF-RELIANCE
     George W. Maxey
15. THE VALUES OF THE NON-INDIAN   126
     WORLD
     Ed McGaa
16. SPORTS MIRROR AMERICAN   133
     VALUES
     Robert J. Bueter
17. OUR DOMINANT CULTURAL   141
     VALUES
     Cora Dubois

Chapter V: AMERICAN RELIGIOUS VALUES
18. RELIGION AND AMERICA'S   151
     MORAL CRISIS
     Eugene B. Borowitz
19. WHATEVER BECAME OF SIN?   159
     Karl Menninger
20. SPORTS AND RELIGION   165
     Cornish Rogers
21. AMERICA'S CIVIL RELIGION   171
     Robert N. Bellah

Chapter VI: WHAT IS PATRIOTISM?
22. WHAT'S HAPPENED TO   184
     PATRIOTISM?
     Max Rafferty
23. WHO IS LOYAL TO AMERICA?   193
     Henry Steele Commager
24. THE PRAGMATICS OF   200
     PATRIOTISM
     Robert A. Heinlein
25. WE NEED A NEW KIND OF   208
     PATRIOTISM
     Ralph Nader

Chapter VII: WHAT AMERICA NEEDS
26. DEVELOPING VALUES IN A   217
     VALUELESS SOCIETY
     Charles W. Anderson

27. WHAT IS RIGHT WITH AMERICA   227
     George S. Benson
28. AMERICAN VALUES IN A   234
     REVOLUTIONARY WORLD
     Warren Bryan Martin
29. WHO WILL SPEAK FOR AMERICA?   244
     Earl L. Butz

SELECTED PERIODICAL BIBLIOGRAPHY   254

ORGANIZATIONS TO CONTACT   260

TABLE OF EXERCISES

1. Ranking American Values   25

2. Distinguishing Between Fact and Opinion   50

3. Case Study: Economic Democracy   77

4. Distinguishing Between Bias and Reason   109

5. Ranking American Heroes   122

6. Recognizing Ethnocentric Statements   148

7. Determining Sin   181

8. Ability to Empathize   214

9. Understanding Stereotypes   252

A major emphasis of this book is on critical thinking skills. Discussion exercises included after readings are not laborious writing assignments. They are included to stimulate class discussion and individual critical thinking.

INTRODUCTION

The purpose of this book, and the **Opposing Viewpoints Series** as a whole, is to present the reader with alternative points of view on complex and sensitive issues.

Perhaps the best way to inform oneself is to analyze the positions of those who are regarded as experts and well studied on the issues. Every reader will approach this book with some opinions of his own on the issues debated within it. However, the educated and well informed person should be able to recognize not only his arguments but those with whom he disagrees, for if one does not completely understand his opponent's point of view he really does not fully understand his own.

A pitfall to avoid in considering alternative points of view is to regard one's own point of view as being merely common sense and the most rational stance, and the point of view of others as being only opinion and naturally wrong. It may be that their opinion is correct and that yours is in error.

Another pitfall to avoid in seeking the best solution when considering controversial issues, is that of closing your mind to the opinions of those whose views differ from yours. The best way to approach a dialogue is to make your primary purpose that of understanding the mind and arguments of the other person and not that of enlightening him with your solutions and convincing him of their correctness.

It is the editor's hope that the reader of this book will enjoy a deeper understanding of the issues debated and will appreciate the complexity of even seemingly simple issues when good and honest men disagree. This awareness is particularly important in a democratic society such as ours, where men enter into public debate to determine the common good. People with whom you disagree should not be regarded as enemies, but rather as friends who suggest a different path to a common goal.

1

I would also like to caution the reader about being unwilling to take a stand on an issue because of a lack of information. That is an excuse and not a reason. One never has enough information. However, one should always be ready to form an opinion from the facts at hand. One should also remain flexible and be able to alter his opinion when new facts indicate that this is necessary.

1 CHAPTER

WHAT DOES AMERICA STAND FOR?

Readings
1. **The American Character**
   J. W. Fulbright
2. **The Bible of Americanism**
   Daniel L. Marsh

THE AMERICAN CHARACTER

J. W. Fulbright

J. W. Fulbright was, until 1973, the senior senator from Arkansas and Chairman of the Senate Foreign Relations Committee. He was born in Sumner, Missouri, in 1905. He holds an A.B. from the University of Arkansas, an A.B. and an M.A. from Oxford University, and an L.L.D. from George Washington University. He was first elected to Congress in 1943 after serving as President of the University of Arkansas. Among his publications are **Prospects for the West**, **Old Myths and New Realities**, and **The Arrogance of Power**.

As you read try to answer the following questions:

1. Why does Mr. Fullbright believe we need a national self-examination?
2. How has Puritanism complicated our national life?
3. How has the frontier helped shape our national character?
4. In the author's opinion, what must be done to overcome hatred and bigotry in our national life?

J. W. Fulbright, "The American Character," **Vital Speeches of the Day**, January 1, 1964, page 164-67. Reprinted with permission.

A National Self-Examination

I believe that our society, though in most respects decent, civilized, and humane, is not, and has never been, entirely so. Our national life, both past and present has also been marked by a baleful and incongruous strand of intolerance and violence.

It is in evidence all around us. It is in evidence in the senseless and widespread crime that makes the streets of our great cities unsafe. It is in evidence in the malice and hatred of extremist political movements. And it is in evidence in the cruel bigotry of race that leads to such tragedies as the killing of Negro children in a church in Alabama.

We must ask ourselves many questions about this element of barbarism in a civilized society. We must ask ourselves what its sources are, in history and in human nature. We must ask ourselves whether it is the common and inevitable condition of man or whether it can be overcome. And if we judge that it can be overcome, we must ask ourselves why we Americans have not made greater progress in doing so.... Finally, and most important, we must ask ourselves what we must do, and how and when, to overcome hatred and bigotry and to make America as decent and humane a society as we would like it to be.

I do not pretend to be able to answer these questions. I do suggest, however, that the conditions of our time call for a national self-examination although the process may be a long and difficult and painful one. I further suggest and most emphatically, that if such a national self-examination is to be productive it must be conducted in a spirit of tolerance rather than anger, serenity rather than guilt, and Christian charity rather than crusading moralism.

We might begin our reflections about ourselves by an examination of the effects of crusading self-righteousness, in the history of Western civilization and in our own society.

Moral Absolutism and the Spirit of Democracy

Moral absolutism — righteous, crusading, and intolerant — has been a major force in the history of

Western civilization. Whether religious or political in form, movements of crusading moralism have played a significant and usually destructive role in the evolution of western societies. Such movements, regardless of the content of their doctrines, have all been marked by a single characteristic: The absolute certainty of their own truth and virtue. Each has regarded itself as having an exclusive pipeline to heaven, to God, or to a deified concept of history — or whatever is regarded as the ultimate source of truth. Each has regarded itself as the chosen repository of truth and virtue and each has regarded all nonbelievers as purveyors of falsehood and evil.

Reprinted by permission of The Minneapolis Star and Roy Justus.

6

Absolutist movements are usually crusading movements. Free as they are from any element of doubt as to their own truth and virtue, they conceive themselves to have a mission of spreading the truth and destroying evil. They consider it to be their duty to regenerate mankind, however little it may wish to be regenerated. The means which are used for this purpose, though often harsh and sometimes barbaric, are deemed to be wholly justified by the nobility of the end. They are justified because the end is absolute and there can be no element of doubt as to its virtue and its truth.

Thus it is that in the name of noble purposes men have committed unspeakable acts of cruelty against one another. The medieval Christians who burned heretics alive did not do so because they were cruel and sadistic; they did it because they wished to exorcise evil and make men godly and pure. The Catholic and Protestant armies which inflicted upon Europe 30 years of death and destruction in the religious wars of the 17th century did not do so because they wished anyone harm; on the contrary, they did it for the purpose of saving Christendom from sin and damnation.

In our time the crusading movements have been political rather than religious, but their doctrines have been marked by the same conviction of absolute truth and the same zeal to perpetuate it. Thus the German Nazis, with their fervent belief in a primitive racial myth, murdered 6 million Jews in their zeal to elevate mankind by ridding it of a race that they deemed venal and inferior. Similarly, the Russian Communists under Stalin, who as Djilas writes, was a man capable of destroying nine-tenths of the human race to make happy the one-tenth — killed millions of their own people and consigned countless others to the slave labor camps of Siberia in order to pave the way for a society in which all men should be equal and happy and free....

The strand of fanaticism and violence has been a major one in western history. But it has not been the only one, nor has it been the dominant one in most western societies. The other strand of Western civilization, conceived in ancient Greece and Rome and revived in the European age of reason, has been one of tolerance and moderation, of empiricism and practicality. Its doctrine has been democracy, a radically different kind of doctrine whose one absolute is the denial of absolutes and of the messianic spirit. The core of the democratic idea is the element of doubt as to the ability of any man or any movement to perceive ultimate truth. Accordingly, it has fostered societies in which the individual is left free to pursue truth and virtue as he imperfectly perceives them, with a different, and quite possibly superior, set of values.

Democratic societies have by no means been free of self-righteousness and the crusading spirit. On the contrary, they have at times engaged in great crusades to spread the gospel of their own ideology. Indeed, no democratic nation has been more susceptible to this tendency than the United States, which in the past generation has fought one war to ''make the world safe for democracy,'' another to achieve nothing less than the unconditional surrender of its enemies, and even now finds it possible to consider the plausibility of total victory over communism in a thermonuclear war.

It is clear that democratic nations are susceptible to dogmatism and the crusading spirit. The point, however, is that this susceptibility is not an expression but a denial of the democratic spirit. When a free nation embarks upon a crusade for democracy, it is caught up in the impossible contradiction of trying to use force to make men free. The dogmatic and crusading spirit in free societies is an antidemocratic tendency, a lingering vestige of the strand of dogmatism and violence in the Western heritage.

> **When a free nation embarks upon a crusade for democracy, it is caught up in the impossible contradiction of trying to use force to make men free.**

The Influence of Puritanism

For a number of complex historical reasons, while most of Europe remained under absolute monarchs and an absolute church, England evolved very gradually into a pluralistic society under a constitutional government. By the time of the establishment of the English

8

colonies in the New World, the evolution toward constitutional democracy was well advanced. The process quickly took hold in the North American colonies and their evolution toward democracy outspaced that of the mother country. This was the basic heritage of America — a heritage of tolerance, moderation, and individual liberty that was implanted from the very beginnings of European settlement in the New World. America has quite rightly been called a nation that was born free.

There came also to the New World the Puritans, a minor group in England who became a major force in American life. Their religion was Calvinism, an absolutist faith with a stern moral code promising salvation for the few and damnation for the many. The intolerant, witch-hunting Puritanism of 17th century Massachusetts was not a major religious movement in America. It eventually became modified and as a source of ethical standards made a worthy contribution to American life. But the Puritan way of thinking, harsh and intolerant, permeated the political and economic life of the country and became a major secular force in America. Coexisting uneasily with our English heritage of tolerance and moderation, the Puritan way of thinking has injected an absolutist strand into American thought — a strand of stern moralism in our public policy and in our standards of personal behavior.

The Puritan way of thinking has had a powerful impact on our foreign policy. It is reflected in our traditional vacillation between self-righteous isolation and total involvement and in our attitude toward foreign policy as a series of idealistic crusades rather than as a continuing defense of the national interest..It is reflected in some of the most notable events of our history: in the unnecessary war with Spain, which was spurred by an idealistic fervor to liberate Cuba and ended with our making Cuba an American protectorate; in the war of 1917, which began with a national commitment to "make the world safe for democracy" and ended with our repudiation of our own blueprint for a world order of peace and law; in the radical pacifism of the interwar years which ended with our total involvement in a conflict in which our proclaimed objective of "unconditional surrender" was finally achieved by dropped atomic bombs on Hiroshima and Nagasaki.

9

Throughtout the 20th century American foreign policy has been caught up in the inherent contradiction between our English heritage of tolerance and accommodation and our Puritan heritage of crusading righteousness....

The danger of any crusading movement issues from its presumption of absolute truth. If the premise is valid, then all else follows. If we know, with absolute and unchallengeable certainty, that a political leader is traitorous, or that he is embarked upon a course of certain ruin for the Nation, then it is our right, indeed our duty, to carry our opposition beyond constitutional means and to remove him by force or even murder. The premise, however, is not valid. We do not know, nor can we know, with aboslute certainty that those who disagree with us are wrong. We are human and therefore fallible, and being fallible, we cannot escape the element of doubt as to our own opinions and convictions. This, I believe, is the core of the democratic spirit. When we acknowledge our own fallibility, tolerance, and compromise become possible and fanaticism becomes absurd.

The Influence of the Frontier

Before I comment on recent events, it is necessary to mention another major factor in the shaping of the American national character. That factor is the experience of the frontier, the building of a great nation out of a vast wilderness in the course of a single century. The frontier experience taught us the great value of individual initiative and self-reliance in the development of our resources and of our national economy. But the individualism of the frontier, largely untempered by social and legal restraints, has also had an important influence on our political life and on our personal relations. It has generated impatience with the complex and tedious procedures of law and glorified the virtues of direct individual action. It has instilled in us an easy familiarity with violence and vigilante justice. In the romanticized form in which it permeates the television and other mass media, the mythology of the frontier conveys the message that killing a man is not bad as long as you don't shoot him in the back, that violence is only reprehensible when its purpose is bad and that in fact it is commendable and glorious when it is perpetrated by good men for a good purpose....

10

The mythology of the frontier, the moral absolutism of our Puritan heritage, and of course, other factors which I have not mentioned, have injected a strand of intolerance and violence into American life. This violent tendency lies beneath the surface of an orderly, law-abiding, democratic society, but not far beneath the surface. When times are normal, when the country is prosperous at home and secure in its foreign relations, our violent and intolerant tendencies remain quiescent and we are able to conduct our affairs in a rational and orderly manner. But in times of crisis, foreign or domestic, our underlying irrationality breaks through to become a dangerous and disruptive force in our national life....

> **The mythology of the frontier, the moral absolutism of our Puritan heritage...have injected a strand of intolerance and violence into American life.**

Suspicion and Hatred in America Today

It is not at all surprising that the underlying tendencies toward violence and crusading self-righteousness have broken through the surface and become a virulent force in the life and politics of the postwar era. They have not thus far been the dominant force because the Nation has been able to draw on the considerable resources of wisdom, patience, and judgment which are the core of our national heritage and character. The dominance of reason, however, has been tenuous and insecure and on a number of occasions in these years of crisis we have come close to letting our passions shape critical decisions of policy.

American politics in the postwar period have been characterized by a virulent debate between those who counsel patience and reason and those who, in their fear and passion, seem ever ready to plunge the Nation into conflict abroad and witch hunts at home....

The voices of suspicion and hate have been heard throughout the land. They were heard a decade ago,

when statesmen, private citizens, and even high-rank-
ing members of the Armed Forces were charged with
treason, subversion, and communism, because they
had disagreed with or somehow displeased the Senator
from Wisconsin, Mr. McCarthy. They are heard today
when extremist groups do not hesitate to call a former
President or the Chief Justice of the United States a
traitor and a Communist. They are heard in the mail
which U.S. Senators receive almost daily charging them
with communism or treason because they voted for the
foreign aid bill or for the nuclear test ban treaty.

If I may, I should like to read a section of a letter
which I recently received from a person called John
Haller of Greenville, Pa., who writes on stationery
carrying the letterhead, "In Defense of the Constitution." The letter is not atypical. It reads, in part, as
follows:

> "Just heard on the news that you are defending the
> wheat sale to Russia and are for giving them credit at
> the American taxpayers(') expense.
>
> "For some time now I have been checking your
> record and find that you would make a better Commun-
> ist than you make an American. Any proposals that
> would protect America or our free-enterprise system
> are opposed by you and any proposals that would help
> our enemies are given your wholehearted support. Your
> famous memorandum is a disgrace and you are a traitor
> to the Constitution."

This malice and hatred which have become a part of
our politics cannot be dismissed as the normal excesses
of a basically healthy society. They have become far too
common. They are beyond the pale of normal political
controversy in which honest men challenge each
other's motives and integrity. The excesses of the
extremists in our country have created an intolerable
situation in which we must all guard our words and the
expression of an unorthodox point of view is an extraordinary act of courage....

We Must Revive and Strengthen the Central Core of Our National Heritage

What is to be done? What must we do to overcome
hatred and bigotry in our national life?...

We will, and should, continue to have controversy and debate in our public life. But we can reshape the character of our controversies and conduct them as the honest differences of honest men in quest of a consensus. We can come to recognize that those who disagree with us are not necessarily attacking us but only our opinions and ideas. Above all, we must maintain the element of doubt as to our own convictions, recognizing that it was not given to any man to perceive ultimate truth and that, however unlikely it may seem, there may in fact be truth or merit in the views of those who disagree with us....

Furthermore, if we are to overcome violence and bigotry in our national life, we must alter some of the basic assumptions of American life and politics. We must recognize that the secular puritanism which we have practiced, with its principles of absolute good, absolute evil, and intolerance of dissent, has been an obstacle to the practice of democracy at home and the conduct of an effective foreign policy. We must recognize that the romanticized cult of the frontier, with its glorification of violence and of unrestrained individualism, is a childish and dangerous anachronism in a nation which carries the responsibility of the leadership of the free world in the nuclear age.

Finally, we must revive and strengthen the central core of our national heritage, which is the legacy of liberty, tolerance, and moderation that came to us from the ancient world through a thousand years of English history and three centuries of democratic evolution in North America. It is this historic legacy which is the best and the strongest of our endowments. It is our proper task to strengthen and cultivate it in the years ahead. If we do so, patiently and faithfully, we may arrive before too long at a time when the voices of hate will no longer be heard in our land.

THE BIBLE OF AMERICANISM

Daniel L. Marsh

> This reading originated as a speech delivered at a dinner of the National Association of Mutual Savings in New York City, May 7, 1942. At that time Dr. Marsh was the president of Boston University.

Reflect on the following questions while you read:

1. Why does the author feel it is important to have a "Bible of Americanism"?
2. What are the seven books of the "Bible of Americanism"? Why was each chosen?
3. How do you think J. W. Fulbright, the author of Reading One, would react to this reading?

Daniel L. Marsh, "The American Canon," **Vital Speeches of the Day**, June 15, 1942, page 524-29. Reprinted with permission.

"Why is it that we do not have something to which every American can give allegiance?" If you ask a member of a religious organization for the source of his authority, no matter whether he is Roman Catholic or Protestant — Methodist, Congregationalist, Episcopalian — he always will name the Bible as the source of his faith. The Hebrew will date his religion back to the Old Testament; the Christian, to the Old Testament and New Testament; and they will say that the canonical scriptures contain the authoritative rule of their faith and practice.

So I said to myself: "What canonical scriptures of Americanism are there that correspond in patriotism to the Bible in religion?" Then, upon my own account, I started out to discover them. I did not say much about it, but I kept on working at it in odds and ends of time for some 20 years, and in the course of that time, I read an enormous number of speeches and papers of one kind and another....

In the course of my study I kept sifting out, applying my own canonical rules to ascertain whether the document really could be classified as part of the Bible of Americanism. Would a particular document stand the canonical test? Could it become a part of the authoritative rule of American patriotism? In the course of study, I selected seven documents. So far as my own judgment goes, there is no eighth. Then, just to carry out the whimsical notion I had, and to add a little to the interest of it, I gave them certain scriptural connotations. I have the Genesis of American Democracy; the Exodus; our Book of the Law; our Major Prophecy; the Psalm of Americanism; the Gospel of Americanism, and the Epistle to the Americans — those seven. I have not found an eighth. I have thought that if we could rear a generation of Americans who would be intelligent concerning those seven, and the conditions of the times out of which they grew, the historical background and implications of them, we would have a body of intelligent patriots. We would give our allegiance to something that was fundamental in democracy. For, in a democracy it is a great deal harder to focus loyalties than it is in a totalitarian system. In a totalitarian state you precisely focus your loyalties upon a person, and you yield your allegiance to the person, In Nazism it is to Hitler; in Fascist Italy it is to Mussolini, and in Communism, it is to Stalin; but

15

when you come to a democracy, if you are going to have an intelligent democracy perpetuated for the future, you will focus your loyalties upon a set of ideals, and you will yield your allegiance to a set of ideas and ideals.

So, we must have an intelligent comprehension of the ideas and ideals that underlie our American democracy. I hold we have them in these seven documents. Let us look at them very quickly.

Genesis: The Mayflower Compact

First of all, the Genesis of our American Democracy is in the Mayflower Compact....

By 1620, the little band in Holland decided that they did not wish to stay there. They did not want their children to become Dutch, and did not like the worldly surroundings, so they made plans to go to America. They managed to get a charter allowing them to settle in Virginia — they expected to land no further north than the Hudson River. They had enormous courage. They had not only the actual hardships of a long voyage, but they were told things which they had no reason to disbelieve, which were even worse than the actualities. For instance, they were told that the savages would capture these white people and bind them to a stake. Then, while they still lived, they would cut out steaks and chops from them and broil the steaks and chops before the eyes of the victims. Nevertheless, they came.

It is an interesting story as to how they got started, trying this and that until the Speedwell and Mayflower groups were formed. The first land they sighted in November, 1620, was what we now call the tip of Cape Cod at Provincetown.

Before they landed, they found they were off their course. They were far north of where they intended to land. Some of the persons they had recruited in London were impatient with the restraints imposed by the leaders of the Pilgrims, and said, "When we land, we will do as we please, for here nobody has authority over us." And they were right. But when the leaders of the Pilgrim band heard this, they assembled all the adult

16

males except two (who were sick) in the cabin of the Mayflower, and, using Miles Standish's sea chest as a desk, they then and there drew up the first written compact by which any group of people upon earth ever agreed to govern themselves. That Mayflower Compact is the Genesis of American democracy....

> In the name of God, Amen. We whose names are underwritten,...having undertaken, for the glory of God, and advancement of the Christian faith, and honor of our king and country, a voyage to plant the first colony in the northern parts of Virginia, do by these presents solemnly and mutually in the presence of God, and one of another, covenant and combine ourselves together into a civil body politic for our better ordering and preservation.

The Mayflower Compact, September 11, 1620

Exodus: The Declaration of Independence

We come to the Exodus — the going out from the land of tyranny and bondage to the Promised Land of liberty and self-government. No matter by which nation the different colonies were formed, it was not long until they all came under the control of England. By 1670 persecutions and oppressions had begun; by 1760, life was almost intolerable. George III had come to the throne. George III was young, only 22 years old; he was dull, stupid, uneducated, arrogant, bigoted, bull-headed, and finally, crazy. His mother had dinned into his ears the dictum, "George, be King!" He accepted the then prevailing philosophy that a colony existed for the enrichment of the mother country. He saw an opportunity to get money to carry on his European wars; and by 1774, the colonies could endure it no longer, so they called a Congress to meet in Philadelphia in September of that year.

They met as Englishmen to defend their rights as Englishmen. They drew up a letter which they addressed to their King, and the King refused to receive

it. When they adjourned, they adjourned as Englishmen to reconvene the following May as Englishmen for
the redress of grievances as Englishmen. But before
they met in May 1775, the sod of Lexington Green had
soaked up the first blood shed for American independence, and at Concord,

> By the rude bridge that arched the flood,
> Their flag to April's breeze unfurled,
> Here once the embattled farmers stood,
> And fired the shot heard 'round the world.

Although they met as Englishmen, it was not long
until they saw that there were other rights than those of
Englishmen which they had to defend, so, by June of
1776 there was introduced into Congress a resolution
that "these United Colonies are, and of rights ought to
be, free and independent states." Then Congress appointed a committee of five men consisting of
Jefferson, Adams, Franklin, Sherman, and Livingston,
to draft a Declaration of Independence. They thought
that a decent regard for the opinion of mankind would
require them to tell the world why they were going to
war. The committee designated Jefferson to draft the
Declaration. He had a reputation for a felicitous style
and a facile pen.

Jefferson — handsome, tall, democratic, a lawyer
from Virginia, red-headed, with a fine literary style —
sat down in his room upon the second floor of the little
lodging house at the corner of 7th and Market Streets in
Philadelphia, and in one half day, without looking at
either pamphlet or book, wrote the Declaration of
Independence — our great national symbol, the Exodus
of American democracy....

Book of Law: The Constitution

We come quickly to our Book of the Law. Of course,
you would know at once that that which corresponds to
the great Mosaic code in the Old Testament is the
Constitution of the United States.

In American history, between the ending of the
Revolutionary War and the adoption of the Constitution
of the United States, there was practical anarchy in
this country. The colonists had been held together
during the war by their fear of the British Redcoat, but

as soon as he was withdrawn, they feared each other more than anything else, and they were especially afraid of a strongly centralized government. There were 13 different states, and those who could see beyond the then immediate present, knew that there was developing upon these shores, 13 jangling, jarring, jealous nations.

As a matter of fact, when England made peace with the colonies, she named all of the 13 states separately in the treaty of peace. Congress had no power. There was no Chief Executive to enforce legislation that Congress adopted. Congress would ask the states to do certain things like appropriating tax moneys, and the states would refuse. Congress issued money, and the people in derision plastered the walls of their houses with it. It was worthless; credit was gone. The soldiers demanded pay, and Congress had no money. The army actually besieged the building where Congress was sitting in Philadelphia, and in terror Congress fled to Princeton and then to New York, where it remained until the Constitution was adopted.

In this period certain wiser heads like George Washington, Benjamin Franklin, James Madison, and Alexander Hamilton, advised the calling of a Constitutional Convention, which met in Philadelphia, May 5, 1787, and remained in session until September 17 of the same year.

I give it to you as my calm and deliberate judgment (I speak carefully as a student of history) that I do not know anywhere in the story of the onward movement of the children of men, any other gathering that can compare with this Constitutional Convention for a self-effacing, disinterested devotion to the cause which had brought them together. There was no lust for the limelight. There was no self-interest to serve. Those men had in mind only one thing — the preservation of the Union with the liberties which had been won upon the field of battle, and in handing the blessings on to posterity....

Note how ours is a government of laws; and when you become acquainted with it and with its implications, I swear no one then will wish to scrap what we have for some uncertain figment of the imagination.

> **We the people of the United States, in order to form a more perfect Union, establish justice, insure domestic tranquility, provide for the common defense, promote the general welfare, and secure the blessings of liberty to ourselves and our posterity, do ordain and establish this CONSTITUTION for the United States of America.**

Constitution of the United States, September 17, 1787

In the Mosaic code you have Ten Commandments. The American counterpart of those Ten Commandments are the first ten Amendments to the Constitution of the United States. We call it our Bill of Rights. The Constitution could never have been adopted if the leaders had not promised that as soon as it was adopted, they would adopt the Bill of Rights as the first ten Amendments. Of course, they were adopted, and as soon as they were adopted they became a part of the Constitution. Some people draw a thin line of distinction between the Constitution and the Amendments, but in reality as soon as an amendment is adopted, it becomes a part of the Constitution just as much as any other part of the Constitution.

Those ten Amendments are like the Ten Commandments of the Mosaic Code, with this difference: that the Mosaic Ten Commandments issue their "Thou shalt not's" to the people, while our Ten Commandments issue their "Thou shalt not's" to the government. In our case that Bill of Rights protects our fundamental freedoms....

Prophecy: Washington's Farewell Address

We pass quickly to our Major Prophecy. We have had many prophets and many prophecies, but I hold that the greatest prophet we ever had — in the true sense of the word prophet (one who is a forthteller — people generally have thought of a prophet as a fore-teller, but he is a forthteller, one who speaks forth great truths) was George Washington; and his major prophecy was his Farewell Address.

George Washington becomes our founder more truly than most nations can point to any man as their founder. He was a great man. Certain biographical and historical "debunkers" have tried to bring him down to the common level, but after they have done their worst, George Washington still stands forth as majestic as Mount Hood, his patriotism unassailed, and as yet unapproached. George Washington was endowed by nature and Providence with that something which gave him the dignity, the mental power, and the military sagacity and authority to become the Father of the American nation....

This great man with limbs of oak, this great man with the mountain mind, and the crystal soul, serves one term and is re-elected for another term. He could have been unanimously elected for the third term, but he chose not to stand for third term. Then, deciding he should not stand for the third term, he thought that he ought to tell his fellow Americans why, so he issued his Farewell Address. Many people have talked about a single phrase in that Farewell Address, to the effect "we should not enter into entangling foreign alliances," and bandied the words about so much during the debate over the League of Nations, some people think his warning was all that was in the address. Those words are not there. Washington did not say anything about "entangling foreign alliances." He said that we should not entangle our fortunes with European ambition and caprice. He was no isolationist. He entered into treaties with foreign nations. He did warn us against baiting and irritating certain foreign nations. But he had many other things in that Farewell Address.

He said, for instance, that a nation ought to preserve its credit, and that it ought never in times of peace to incur national debt. A nation ought to pay its way as it goes in times of peace, so that in an emergency of war, it will be able to finance itself. He also said that we should not stir up disunion. He pled against the deep damnation of disunion — arraying one class against another. He pled for education. He knew that whenever a people undertook to do their own dictatorship, they assumed the obligations, as well as the privilege of the function, and they could not govern themselves unless education were widely diffused, and the electorate were intelligent. He said many things in that speech which ought to be read today. The Farewell Address is our Major Prophecy.

> **Of all the dispositions and habits which lead to political prosperity, religion and morality are indispensable supports.**

Washington's Farewell Address, September 17, 1796

Psalms: The Star Spangled Banner

We come quickly to the Psalm of Americanism...the Star Spangled Banner.

Francis Scott Key, in that song, is not narrowly nationalistic at all, simply fervently patriotic. He does not glorify war. He uses the imagery of battle, but uses it only to glorify the flag. It is the flag, not the war, that is glorified.

There is a philosophy of colors: White stands for the blending of all the virtues; blue, because it is the color of the heavens, stands for honesty, truth, and purity. The stars represent ideals, as well as the states; and red is the sign of courage.

May I say to you that, aesthetically considered, without any reference at all to the things for which it stands, the aesthetic arrangement of the length in proportion to the width, the arrangement of the little square heaven of blue and the stars in it, and the stripes — that flag is the most beautiful flag which floats anywhere under the whole canopy of Heaven.

But we honor it not for its aesthetic value, and the song glorifies it not for its aesthetic beauty, but because of that for which it stands — a pledge that liberty shall prevail, that righteousness shall be done, that justice shall be meted out wherever the flag floats. Its stars laughing down their delightful light by day and night, and its stripes stroked in ripples of white and of red, are the symbol of our Government, and that is why we honor it. That is the Psalm of Americanism.

Gospel: Lincoln's Second Inaugural Address

I move quickly and briefly to the Gospel of Americanism. This would have to come out of the heart of the savior of the American Union — and who is the savior of the American Union? Only one person can qualify for that position — Abraham Lincoln....

I hold that the second inaugural address of Abraham Lincoln is the greatest literary production that has ever come from an American hand. You have to get the condition of the times in mind to appreciate it at its real worth. The Civil War has been wallowing its bloody way across the heart of the Nation for four years. The end is near at hand. Lincoln's own party in the North is demanding revenge. Everywhere, lust, hate, and spite — an eye for an eye, a tooth for a tooth; everywhere recriminations and calling of names. Here comes this man whose whole history has been one of freedom from bigotry and intolerance. Lincoln would not be caught up in hysteria that would prompt him to burn a flag of a nation with which we technically are not at war, or call everybody with whom he did not agree a Fifth Columnist, a Nazi, or anything else. Lincoln was broad-minded and great-hearted.

He now is ready to deliver his second inaugural address. All that morning, that 4th of March, 1865, it has been drizzling rain. The crowd is out there in front of the Capitol in Washington. Lincoln comes onto the east portico of the Capitol. He is tall, gaunt, his shoulders stooped as though the burden of his country's woes were heavier than he could bear; his eyes sunken as though the knuckles of sorrow had pushed them back into their sockets.

As he begins to speak, voice high with emotion, there is a rift in the cloud, and a sun-beam falls straight upon Lincoln. The clouds gradually roll back until the

With malice toward none; with charity for all...

Lincoln's Second Inaugural Address, March 4, 1865

whole crowd is flooded with light. Lincoln delivers his short inaugural. It is like a page torn out of the prophecy of Isaiah, freighted with moral intensity, talking about God, then he comes to that last great sentence — I think the greatest in American literature

23

— "With malice toward none; with charity for all; with firmness in the right, as God gives us to see the right, let us strive on to finish the work we are in; to bind up the nation's wounds; to care for him who shall have borne the battle, and for his widow and his orphans — to do all which may achieve and cherish a just and lasting peace among ourselves and with all nations." That is the Gospel of Americanism.

Epistle: Wilson's, "The Road Away From Revolution"

I have but one more. It is the Epistle to the Americans. Many things clamored for inclusion in "The American Canon;" but, as I went on sifting, it seemed to be that there was one and only one, and that was the last article Woodrow Wilson ever wrote, his article entitled "The Road Away from Revolution."...

Woodrow Wilson, trained in the South and North, historian, college professor, university president, Governor of a state, President of the United States, increasing in strength with each new responsibility and never losing the ideals that he inherited from his Presbyterian preacher father, — Woodrow Wilson carried the nation through the First World War. War over — he retired, a broken man.

In 1923, the Spring of the year, Wilsom seems to have had a premonition of the trouble which came on the country in 1929 and following, and he expressed a wish to write an article to save his country, if he could, from what he saw ahead....

Keep in mind that Wilson was a capitalist and believed in the capitalistic system. He was afraid of what he saw ahead and was trying to forewarn his fellow Americans so that this system under which America had prospered and become great, might remain unimpaired. He pled, therefore, that capitalists should use their capital in the service of others. Service — that was the great plea of Wilson. He said that we must introduce the spirit of Jesus and Christianity into our business life, into our commercial and industrial affairs. His article I call an Epistle to the Americans.

Thus I have given you in brief outline what I call "The American Canon," the canonical scriptures of true Americanism.

RANKING AMERICAN VALUES

This exercise will give you an opportunity to discuss with your classmates the values you consider important and the values you believe are considered most important by the majority of Americans.

© King Features Syndicate 1975

Part I

Instructions

STEP 1. The class should break into groups of four to six students, and discuss the meaning of the Hagar cartoon.

STEP 2. Working individually, within each group, each student should rank the values listed below, assigning the number (1) to the value he personally considers most important, the number (2) to the second most important value, and so on, until all the values have been ranked.

STEP 3. Each student should compare his ranking with others in the group, giving the reasons for his ranking.

VALUES TO BE RANKED

_____ financial security

_____ freedom of speech

_____ equality of opportunity

_____ self-reliance

_____ loyalty to country

_____ tolerance of others

_____ freedom of religion

_____ individual initiative

_____ right to private property

_____ government by law and not men

_____ concern for the underdog

_____ fair play

_____ justice

_____ order in society

Part II

Instructions

STEP 1. Working in groups of four to six students, each group should rank the values listed in what the group considers the order of importance to the majority of Americans. Assign the number (1) to the value the group believes is most important to the average American, the number (2) to the second most important value, and so on, until all the values have been ranked.

STEP 2. Each group should compare its ranking with others in the class in a classwide discussion.

CHAPTER

AMERICAN BUSINESS VALUES

Readings
3. **Business is the Source of Our Values**
   Otto A. Bremer
4. **The Businessman's Right to Profit**
   Edward Maher
5. **The Gospel Way and the American Way
   Are Contradictory**
   Eugene C. Bianchi
6. **Competition Is Essential**
   James M. Roche
7. **Capitalism Is Destroying America**
   Tom Christoffel, David Finkelhor
   and Dan Gilbarg
8. **Government Regulations Are Destroying Capitalism**
   Hans F. Sennholz

BUSINESS IS THE SOURCE OF OUR VALUES

Otto A. Bremer

Reverend Bremer is Campus Pastor at the Lutheran Campus Ministry, University of California at Santa Barbara, in Goleta, California. He was recently a Newcomen Society Fellow in Business History at the University of Southern California Graduate School of Business Administration.

Consider the following questions while reading:

1. What is the author's primary claim?
2. How does the author try to support this claim in discussing the family and pension funds?
3. Why do traditional value sources have less influence in our society today, in the author's opinion? Do you agree?
4. If the author's claim is correct, what consequences do you see?

Otto A. Bremer, "Is Business the Source of New Social Values?" **Harvard Business Review**, November-December 1971, pp. 121-26. This reading consists of segments of the original article.

Business is today the most significant force shaping American life and the strongest influence determining the everyday values of the average citizen; the operative values in the management of a corporate enterprise tend to become the operative values in the daily life of society....

The present student generation has grown up with less value input from traditional sources than any previous one. It is also the first to have had a lifelong exposure to nontraditional values through television. My experience with these students has convinced me that, more than any older generation, they are keenly aware of the dominant influence of business on society....

The purpose of this article is to show why I am firmly convinced that the future of our society is going to be determined more by the day-to-day decisions of corporate managers — and the values that dictate these decisions — than by any other single influence. This conclusion is reached after 25 years as a student of business, a pastor to businessmen, and a campus pastor in turbulent Isla Vista....

Business is today the most significant force shaping American life.

Supporting Evidence

Of all our institutions, the family is most vulnerable to the influence of business values spilling over society in general. In my marriage and family counseling I often encounter people who look upon the family as primarily a financial institution — usually without being aware this is happening. Success is judged by the amount of capital accumulation and the expansion of assets. Difficulties, such as divorce and the rejection of younger members, frequently have their roots in the charge that someone is "unproductive" or "does not contribute to family success." Unconditional love, in the traditional, religious sense, has given way in these families to the standards of accountability appropriate to business.

Increasingly, other institutions are adopting business methods and the values that support them, such as efficiency, profitability, productivity, and quantitative criteria. There is no campaign by businessmen to bring this about, but demands to put public schools, universities, social service agencies, and churches on a "sound business basis" are receiving more and more support these days. In most cases I find myself approving, but should we not think long and hard about the future effects? For example, one group of churches is adopting Planning, Programming, Budgeting Systems (PPBS) as its basic administrative tool, and the church "executives" are attending explanatory seminars at the University of Michigan School of Industrial Relations. The present leadership is confident it can modify the assumptions of quantitatively measurable results to include the intangible aims and purposes of religion. Somehow, though, the two seem diametrically opposed.

Think about the way an average citizen invests in a pension fund. The value message he gets from the fund manager is most likely focused at maximizing his return on the investment in financial terms; he watches the fund closely and identifies his future with it. But are there not other returns on this investment, based on other values that are being overridden by the solely economic one? The investor thinks in economic terms about his future because he has been influenced in that direction. But what about his future in terms of a clean environment, racial equality, and individual dignity? There are corporations which further these virtues and make a profit, and corporations which do not further them and make a profit. Why not invest in the former to insure a more "valuable" future? Most people don't think of this because economic values are dominating the others....

The United States has traditionally depended on the interplay of various "value input sources" — farm life, communities, churches, business, eduation, and so on — to shape the values of each individual and, in sum, the values of society. The outcome, on the whole, has been very good. Each institution (or what I am calling value input source) made its contribution, but society — individually and collectively — made the final decision as to which values would prevail....

There has always been the unspoken assumption that no one source will dictate the values of the whole society, that somehow the final mix of generally accepted values will be a balanced combination of the best from all value input sources....

"RELIGIOUS FREEDOM IS MY IMMEDIATE GOAL, BUT MY LONG-RANGE PLAN IS TO GO INTO REAL ESTATE."

Drawing by Donald Reilly; © 1974 The New Yorker Magazine, Inc.

A Competitive Advantage

Today, the foregoing scenario is no longer applicable. In the language of our parallel in economic theory, the competition between the various value input sources has become quite "imperfect." The influence of education, family, community, church, and so on, in forming the values that individuals live by, is greatly diminished, and the influence of business is consequently stronger than ever before.

Think for a moment about what has happened to the traditional value input sources that influenced the everyday life of Mr. John Q. Citizen a generation or two ago:

Agricultural society — Even when people were leaving the farm in large numbers, they did not do so without having internalized some "down-to-earth" values that lasted a lifetime. Farming itself is now a big business, highly mechanized with daily life influenced more by the values of nearby urban centers than by the agricultural routines of the past.

Family — The extended family of the past helped to secure the passing on of values from generation to generation. Today, few children have daily contact with grandparents who, as Margaret Mead says, "cannot conceive of any future for the children than their (the grandparents') own past lives." [1]

Town or community — People are now more apt to experience short, rootless residential stops in innumerable, indistinguishable suburbs than to live in the town where they were born and intend to die; thus, assimilation of community mores is considerably weakened.

Religion — One does not really need the results of the many studies showing that people today look less and less to the churches and synagogues as a source of values. It is obvious that religion is not nearly the integrative and normative force that it once was.

Education — I suspect that most readers of this article can recall an elementary school experience characterized by uncritical transmittal of the values of the American way of life. To be sure, these values were usually seen from the perspective of a white, Anglo-Saxon, Protestant middle class imbued with patriotism and the puritan ethic, but the influence was strong. Today, we are more sensitive to the pluralistic nature of society and less willing to impose the values of the majority.

Direct evidence of the demise of traditional value sources is seen in the attempt of many young people to reestablish meaningful contact with contemporary substitutes for them: mystical cults take the place of organized religion; earth food, ecology action, and closeness to nature substitute for the farm; and communal living replaces the extended family.

While the sources of traditional values decline in influence...the influence of business has not declined and that now, by default, business finds itself with far more influence on society than ever intended — or desired.

THE BUSINESS OF AMERICA IS BUSINESS

President Calvin Coolidge

The Emerging Monopolist

We are all familiar with cases where single institutions have dominated the values of other societies. In fact, many immigrants to the United States from Prussia and elsewhere sought to escape what they called a "military society." Other immigrants remembered with some nostalgia an "agricultural society" in which the farm, as a living ecosystem, was the pervasive model. For some, this nostalgia almost blotted out the fact that they had left their homelands because the domination by agricultural values stifled new ideas and possibilities for industrial development.

Experience taught both the early settlers and later immigrants that one way to safeguard freedom was to be certain that checks and balances were built into the formal and informal structures of American culture. Few concepts are more deeply embedded in our understanding of what the American way of life is all about.

During the past half-century, however, the description of the United States as a "business society" has been used more and more. The designation expresses a positive and appreciative recognition of the success of the business community in contributing to the highest standard of living in the world. But could "business society" also describe a modern counterpart to the church-dominated society of the middle ages or the military societies, both past and present?...

I do not mean to deny the positive influence of business values on society, such as the quality of judging people on the basis of individual competence rather than on wealth, family, or connections. There are many other similiar examples, but these should not lull us into complacency about the value crisis confronting us.

As I stated at the outset of this article, the operative values in the management of a corporate enterprise tend to become the operative values of the average citizen. If this is true, it seems clear that the future will be largely shaped by the business community.

1 **Culture and Commitment: A Study of the Generation Gap** (Garden City, New York, Natural History Press/Doubleday & Company, Inc., 1970), p. 1.

THE BUSINESSMAN'S RIGHT TO PROFIT

Edward Maher

The following reading was originally delivered as a lecture at Georgetown University in August of 1963. At the time Mr. Maher was Vice President of the National Association of Manufacturers. The N.A.M. represents industry's views on national and international problems to the government. It reviews current and proposed legislation and maintains a public relations program representing industry's views on national issues.

Use the following questions to assist you in your reading:

1. What argument does the author make to show that profit taking is morally sound?
2. Does the author think there is such a thing as too much profit?
3. How do a company's profits benefit the consumer? Do you agree with the author's claim?

Edward Maher, ''The Ethical Aftermath of Profit,'' **Vital Speeches of the Day**, September 15, 1963, page 735-36. Reprinted with permission.

People tend to forget that ours is a profit-and-loss system and that even in the average good business year somewhere between 35 and 40 per cent of American corporations lose money. The losers aren't the same every year, of course, because those who lose consistently soon go out of business. But even large and well-known companies are not strangers to loss on occasion over their corporate history.

This is a point I think we need to bear in mind, because the possibility of loss instead of profit is ever-present in the minds of American managers. For many thousands of smaller companies, it looms as a probability rather than a possibility.

Another point which I believe needs to be made is that when management views the profit-and-loss statement it's not only to see what monetary gain might be involved. Management's concern over profit is wider than a mere interest in how much money was made. Profit has specific and vital functions to perform in our economy, such as serving to measure the value the community places on any particular enterprise or as a yardstick of management skill....

I often wonder why business ethics are given so much attention when so little is devoted to exploring ethics in other aspects of our national life.

It seems to me that a discussion of ethics in other areas is needed quite as much as it is in the affairs of business. For instance, what about the ethical considerations involved in political campaign promises, which those who make them know cannot and won't be kept? Or in government fiscal policies which steadily erode the value of the savings people have accumulated? What about the ethical aspects of keeping thousands of unneeded men in unneeded jobs on the railroads, drawing pay for non-existent duties? It seems to me it requires a double standard of ethics to see much difference between this and appropriating the possessions of others by more direct methods. What about the ethics involved in threatening to strike New York City schools, where teachers' salaries are among the highest in the nation, to enforce a demand for still higher salaries against the community as a whole? For that matter, what about the ethics involved in setting up picket lines which interfere with the personal freedom of people to go to their jobs when they don't wish to join in a strike?

There are indeed many places in our national affairs where a review of ethical considerations would be appropriate and constructive. My purpose in digressing to this extent is merely to remind you that it isn't only in the business field where such a review would be useful.

PROFITS AND THE PUBLIC INTEREST

"Profit" is the mainspring of our whole economic structure and one of the greatest instruments for public service ever devised. It is obvious, with a little thought, that the many social responsibilities and public service activities of business today are completely dependent on the vitality of our economic system, which in turn is dependent on the profit motive for its energizing force.

I don't need to dwell on the fact that the profit system brings us great material benefits. No other system in all history has brought such a high standard of living to such a large proportion of the population. It is the chief source of opportunity as well as prosperity for the great mass of our citizens.

Also, we know that profits and freedom go hand in hand. Without the profit motive, some form of compulsion must be used to sustain essential economic activity.

From "Profits and The Public Interest," by Howard J. Morgens, Chairman of The Executive Committee, Board of Directors, the Procter and Gamble Co. Distributed by Americanism Educational League.

Profits and Ethics

In discussing the ethical aspects of profit, I might begin by recalling the Christian precept which holds that men are enjoined by the Creator to utilize to the best of their ability the talents which have been bestowed upon them, not only for the improvement of themselves but of society in general.

Now, not everybody in our society has the ability to initiate, organize and carry on the economic activites by which we live. And many of those who have the ability don't care to use their talents in this fashion. They prefer, perhaps, to be educators, public administrators, labor union officials, or even to take a job somewhere and let someone else worry about finance, production, sales, industrial relations, and competition in the market place.

But those who possess and utilize the ability to organize and create enterprises, small or great, to discover new ways to convert nature's gifts to the service of humanity, to devise means by which greater abundance can be developed, financed and distributed, are certainly no less morally worthy because they choose to follow the path of entrepreneurship.

How do these people we call "entrepreneurs" go about exercising the talents God gave them? First, they assemble the capital necessary to begin a enterprise, either by saving it themselves or by joining with others to accumulate the necessary financing. Then they research and develop a product which they hope will fill some widespread need or want. Then they invest in the building of a plant and in the purchase of machinery. They hire and pay a labor force to turn out the product. They seek a market for it so the plant and labor force can be kept working. And they try, in the face of intense competition, to sell the product at a price that will yield sufficient profit to carry on the business...because without profit the enterprise will falter and die.

It follows logically that if the creation and operation of the business enterprise is ethically and morally sound, profit is also sound from the ethical standpoint, because the making of profit is an essential part of the process. The hope of profit is what motivates the entrepreneur to speculate with his money and his ability in an enterprise of his own rather than seeking a safe spot or a berth where someone else takes all the risks. The entrepreneur speculates on the possibility that the product he develops will be one people will find useful and desirable; on the possibility that he will be able to produce and sell it in sufficient quantity and at a price which will yield a profit; that he will be able to withstand the challenge of competition. The success of his speculation is measured by the profit he makes.

AMERICA'S STRENGTHS

The history of this country makes it clear that those two basic strengths, political stability and the best economic system in the world, have combined to make possible more freedom, more choice, more leisure, and more opportunity for development of self and soul than anywhere else in the world.

John J. Riccardo, President, Chrysler Corporation on March 12, 1971.

Too Much Profit?

This brings up what I think is the nub of the ethical question concerning profits. How much? Some people would say that a percentage of profit beyond a certain arbitrary norm — say 6 per cent on the invest — is exorbitant and therefore ethically indefensible. Others, who understand the operation of the free economic system, contend that there is no such thing as an exorbitant or unwarranted profit. Their reasoning is that when capital can earn a greater return in one form of activity than in others, it is an indication of a growing need on the part of society for the kind of activity that yields a larger return. This larger return will very shortly attract additional capital into that particular field and through increased competition the rate of profit will soon be brought down to about the same level that capital is able to earn elsewhere. Meanwhile, increased supplies of the product or service will become available to meet society's need at the price that reflects the value consumers put on it.

This is a function of profit that people sometimes fail to understand. A higher than normal profit attracts additional capital to where it is needed, and a lower than normal profit chases it from where it is not needed, so that we have a highly flexible system which responds readily to the wants and needs of consumers. Looked at in this light, profits in a sense are wages of capital, and just as necessary a part of the cost of running a business as the compensation paid to employees.

When a man puts the skill of his hands or brain to work everyone concedes his right to get as much as he can for his services either on his own or through collective bargaining. But when this same man puts his property to work by investing it in an enterprise which provides jobs and strength for the country, his return — or his profit on his capital — is considered fair game for the demands of labor and the levies of the tax collector.

From the philosophical standpoint, it must be conceded that the compensation a man gets for his services takes priority over the compensation he gets for the use of his property. And this is the way it actually works out in business, because wages and salaries must be paid before any profits are figured up or any dividend checks written. But just as a man surely will seek the job which pays the most for his talents, so will the capital he owns seek the uses which provide the greatest return. In fact, it's much easier for him to shift his capital than it is to shift himself. He can transfer his capital almost at will from one form of investment to another — from the savings bank to stocks and bonds, from shares in one corporation to shares in another, from stocks to real estate or government securities, or back to the bank....

Profits and the Consumer

Let's turn for a moment to a discussion of what profit means to the consumer. It means that the company earning the higher profit has found ways to produce and distribute goods cheaper than its competition. Its product must carry about the same price in the market place or it wouldn't be getting any orders. Therefore, if it is able to show a greater profit it must be producing more efficiently. It must be using human and other resources with greater skill. Its personnel must be superior, its location better, or its manufacturing techniques more advanced. It is also probable that the highly profitable company is spending more money than its competitors to find and develop new and better products and on machinery and manufacturing techniques which will turn them out at less cost. The employees of the profitable company probably have good wages and fringe benefits, and certainly a greater degree of job security than the employees of companies which are skirting on the thin edge of profitability.

Sooner or later, the high-cost and marginal producers whose profits are low or non-existent must mend their ways, get new blood and new ideas, up-date their manufacturing and distributing methods and turn out products which are closer to the customers' needs and desires. As this happens, price, quality and service competition is likely to intensify, with each company trying to outdo the other in satisfying the consumer. The result is a horn of plenty for consumers, with more and better things for less.

It would be idle to deny that individuals or companies on occasion seek to enhance profits by circumventing the competitive pressures of the market place. Collusion to fix prices, unfair methods of competition, false and misleading advertising, bribery and corruption are by no means unknown in business dealings. Similar shady practices go on in other aspects of our national life.

In business it is not only unethical but illegal to attempt to enhance profits by such practices. We have antitrust laws to prevent monopoly and price-fixing; laws to prevent unfair methods of competition; laws to prevent the mislabeling of goods; laws to guarantee honest weights and measures; laws which prohibit false advertising; laws to safeguard the rights of labor and of stockholders.

All reputable businessmen and business organizations recognize the need for such laws and support them. They also recognize that, human nature being what it is, there will be violators and that such violators must be punished if the health of our economy and our free society is to be preserved. They would hope to see the same rigid application of legal and ethical standards in other areas.

But with respect to profit-making by legitimate

means and in accordance with the operation of our free economic system, businessmen are not in the least in doubt about the ethical nature of their calling. They believe the successful operation of a business is a contribution to the betterment of society and of their fellow men, and that whatever profit is realized is the result of a diligent application of the talents God gave them.

THE GOSPEL WAY AND THE AMERICAN WAY ARE CONTRADICTORY

Eugene C. Bianchi

Dr. Bianchi is associate professor of religion at Emmory University in Atlanta.

The following questions will help you to examine the reading:

1. How are individualism and communal consciousness examples of the tension between capitalism and Christianity?
2. How does the author distinguish between capitalist individualism and healthy individualism?
3. What other examples does the author use to point out the contradictions between capitalism and Christianity?
4. Why does the author feel that foundational American ideals are compatible with Christianity?

Eugene C. Bianchi, "Capitalism and Christianity Revisited," **The Christian Century**, December 6, 1972, pp. 1241-44. Copyright 1972 Christian Century Foundation. Reprinted by permission from the December 6, 1972 issue of **The Christian Century**.

Individualism Versus Community

I would like to point out some of the incompatibilities between gospel Christianity and capitalism as we know them. By capitalism, I mean not simply an economic system but the great productive network that spreads over our social, political and cultural life. That is, I understand capitalism as a total environment in which we are reared and conditioned.... I maintain that certain general but essential orientations of the Gospel Way and the American Way are contradictory.....

Capitalism, as an economic system geared mainly to maximizing profits, fosters intense individualism. On the other hand, the core beliefs of the Judeo-Christian tradition stress communal consciousness. Thus, to say that men won't exercise productive initiative without the profit motive to drive them solves nothing *religiously.* For the dangling carrot seems to lure them on toward greater self-centeredness, toward ever more ruthless manipulation of nature and fellow humans for personal (or at best familial) aggrandizement. Corporations are not community-oriented; they are utilitarian aggregates of individuals organized for maximizing *private* profits. The criterion for determining one's self-identity necessarily implies invidiousness and material superiority over others — key motivating elements of capitalism's handmaid, the advertising industry. In brief, if capitalism, as we know it, did not create the Hobbsian war of all against all, it certainly cultivates the seeds of such enmity. The self is supreme over against others.

Look now at the Judeo-Christian heritage. As mirrored in pivotal documents and holy personalities, it centers on the creation of community. The Hebrew scriptures stress a social conception of God and man. The covenants between Yahweh and his people emphasize community in which the person of God is extended into communal human relationships. The corporate person of Israel rejected individualism with its glorification and isolation of the self — for example, in the controversy over kingship. The prophets also voice the strong ethical demands of the convenantal pact. They call Israel to turn away from the pursuit of private wealth and power and to renew the covenant of social justice and communal responsibility.

The Gospels carry on this theme of community-building as against the individualistic emphases of the Roman imperial world. The master image of early Christianity is the selfless Jesus who dedicates himself in suffering love to the creation of a new people. The Pauline literature develops this anti-individualism into the establishment of church communities where the common good is uppermost. The community (portrayed in Acts) of brothers and sisters lovingly committed to a corporate ministry of worship and action became a model for Christian living....

There is a healthy kind of individualism — the kind that is resistant to group tyranny and therefore accords with the Christian ideal of community. But capitalist individualism is not concerned about promoting the growth of the person into emotional, intellectual, ethical and cultural fullness; rather, it fosters the development of individual traits only so far as these are useful for maximizing profits. Thus, ironically, capitalist individualism turns into a group despotism under which personal becoming is sacrificed to the external tyrannies of material gain.

Capitalism as we know it puts a high premium on the possession of material goods.... The gospel commands us to share material goods, not to amass them.

But our technocratic capitalism is still destructively rooted in a primitive attitude toward things. Social Darwinism's stress on the "survival of the fittest" has been but slightly muted as American society's dominant tenet. Among us, possession of material goods is still the clearest sign of "fitness." To possess more is to be more worthy as a person. The great majority of our people still cling to the Horatio Alger myth that the goal of life is to make lots of money. This acquisitive spirit is confirmed in the American attitude toward the poor, who are condemned as willful or unwitting failures at becoming individual possessors — that is, in American terms, "persons."...

Capitalism depends on intense competitiveness coupled with overt and covert forms of violence. Family and school inculcate the spirit of rugged individualism, of getting ahead and rising to the top. Whether in athletics, academe, business or profession, competition requires that the neighbor be more or less violently put down. Ethical lip service is paid to the means employed in becoming "successful," while individual responsibility for the humaneness of the means is minimized or eliminated. The compulsion to compete and achieve is all pervasive. In this milieu, to be human is to be violent toward nature, self and others. For only the respectably aggressive will possess goods, status and selfhood.

Abroad, our economic-political-military entanglements assure the spread of competitive violence. Political spheres of influence become vital for economic expansion and financial gain. The cold-war mentality, with its attitude of distrustful rivalry for pre-eminence, can turn into a hot war whenever our politico-economic interests are threatened. That so-called communist countries behave much as we do may help us to assess the world situation, but it does not justify the American style of competitive violence.

That style is a home brew whose ingredients, stirred together over more than two centuries, include the self-righteous notion of "manifest destiny" (with its concomitant racism), a passion for and enslavement to technology, and the all-enveloping ideal of getting rich. The consequences are destructive violence to nature and self and to less advantaged races and classes. Competitive America is raping its land, fouling its air and water for the purpose of making money. Those who compulsively engage in the routine of competition must deny themselves inward growth, for contemplation of spirit or beauty, or yielding to feelings of tenderness, would distract them. Thus they have no compunctions about keeping oppressed groups (e.g., women, blacks) at menial levels to service the competitive machine for the benefit of the master aggressors.

47

Basic American Ideals and Christianity

This picture of our culture is not a balanced one, but I stress the negativities of America because I believe they are now clearly in the ascendancy. The competitive ethos with its undercurrents of violence is diametrically opposed to Judeo-Christian teaching. The Hebrew religious ideal gradually evolved into that of redemptive suffering. Isaiah's "suffering servant" symbolizes Israel's mission to the nations. The prophets not only preached a more just society but exemplified nonviolent forms of resistance. Jesus commanded sensitivity and service to the needs of one's fellow men. The Jesus of the Beatitudes has always stood as a contradiction to the Christ of the Crusades invented by the church.

Our time has seen new models of suffering love in Gandhi, Martin Luther King and others. Their life style of nonviolent, prophetic resistance to the powers of death and injustice offers a singular hope for authentic rebirth in Christianity. But it is doubtful that the entrenched churches will discover the sources of courage and commitment needed to realize this ideal. Perhaps the way of nonviolent resistance will always be that of the few....

> **To possess more is to be more worthy as a person. The great majority of our people still cling to the Horatio Alger myth that the goal of life is to make lots of money.**

How do we as Christians face the contradictions between our milieu and our deepest commitments? Is there a constructive way to pattern a truly Christian life today? Certainly the first need is to recognize our situation — to recognize it at the gut level of our self-perception as struggling Christians in a hostile environment. It is no solution to import other sociopolitical systems which suffer from many of the same defects that mar ours, though they be called socialist or communist. Second, we must admit our daily complicity in oppressive systems and attitudes. This confession, rather than depressing and immobilizing us, can dispose us for the kind of change of heart and action that conduces new life styles.

As for positive action, we can strive through whatever channels are available to re-establish in our national life the principles of the Bill of Rights and the Declaration of Independence. These foundational American ideals are compatible with Christianity, though today they are merely themes for Fourth of July orators. We can also try to revive the better elements of native American populism and at the same time keep ourselves open to new forms of democratic socialism, whether these appear at home or abroad. Finally, we must do our best to incorporate into our own lives the Judeo-Christian tradition of cooperation and equality.

DISTINGUISHING BETWEEN FACT & OPINION

This discussion exercise is designed to promote experimentation with one's ability to distinguish between fact and opinion. It is a fact, for example, that the United States was militarily involved in the Vietnam War. But to say this involvement served the interests of world peace is an opinion or conclusion. Future historians will agree that American soldiers fought in Vietnam, but their interpretations about the causes and consequences of the war will probably vary greatly.

Part I

Instructions

The following statements are taken from readings in this chapter. Consider each statement carefully. Mark **O** for any statement you feel is an opinion or interpretation of the facts. Mark **F** for any statement you believe is a fact. Then discuss and compare your judgments with those of other class members.

O = OPINION
F = FACT

_____1. Business is today the most significant force shaping American life.

_____2. The future of our society is going to be determined more by the day-to-day decisions of corporate managers — and the values that dictate these decisions — than any other single influence.

_____3. Our economic system is a profit and loss system.

_____4. Profit is the mainspring of our whole economic structure and one of the greatest instruments for service ever designed.

_____5. The profit system brings us great material benefits.

_____6. Capitalism puts a high premium on the possession of material goods.

_____7. Corporations are not community-oriented.

_____8. The Judeo-Christian heritage stresses communal relationships.

_____9. The basic principles of the Bill of Rights and the Declaration of Independence are compatible with Christianity.

_____10. Capitalism thrives on competition.

_____11. Our country is preeminent in the world.

_____12. Controlling much of American thought today are intellectual elitists — professors, journalists, artists, bureaucrats.

_____13. Capitalism is destroying America.

_____14. The income structure in America has remained virtually static since 1910.

_____15. Free enterprise no longer exists in America.

_____16. The automobile threatens to destroy our civilization.

_____17. Ours is a society that does not give priority to people and their needs, but to profit.

_____18. Government regulations are destroying capitalism.

_____19. In a system of unhampered economic freedom, a monopolistic market position could be maintained only through efficiency.

_____20. It is inaccurate to call what exists in the U.S. today capitalism.

Part II

Instructions

STEP 1. The class should break into groups of four to six students.

STEP 2. Each small group should try to locate two statements of fact and two statements of opinion in the book.

STEP 3. Each group should choose a student to record its statements.

STEP 4. The class should discuss and compare the small groups' statements.

COMPETITION IS ESSENTIAL

James M. Roche

> The following reading originated as a speech delivered by Mr. Roche to the Executive Club of Chicago in 1971. At the time Mr. Roche was the Chairman of General Motors Corporation. Mr. Roche is also a former chairman of The Automobile Manufacturers Association.

Bring the following questions to your reading:

1. The author cites two premises on which he says everyone can agree. Do you agree?
2. What threat to America does the author warn about?
3. How does the author react to present day criticism of the free enterprise system?

James M. Roche, ''The Competitive System,'' **Vital Speeches of the Day**, May 1, 1971, page 445-48. Reprinted with permission.

The Threat To Our American System of Free Enterprise

Today, then, let me call your attention to a serious, yet subtle, threat to our American system of free enterprise. I would like to discuss this threat, and the personal responsibility it places upon us, as business-men, to help counter it.

There are two premises on which I think we can all agree. *The first is that our country — by almost any measure — is preeminent in the world.* To assert this is not to deny our faults. We are still short of achieving many of our national ideals. But neither should we deny the blessings we enjoy as a nation. Most apparent per-haps is our unmatched material well-being. More im-portant, though, are our high levels of education, health, and individual opportunity, and of course our freedoms, the priceless heritage our history has served to enlarge.

A second premise, like the first, is also too little acknowledged. It is that our free competitive economic system has been essential to the achievement and the preservation of these national endowments.

These beliefs may seem fundamental to us. Never-theless, they are questioned by some people in our society today. Notwithstanding that America is the envy and the aspiration of the world, there are those who maintain our economic system is not the best, and ask is there not a better way. Some who question our society and its achievements are young. Some are well-intentioned. Some are sincere.

But there are others. Their final objectives are not what they first profess. Their beliefs, their purposes, run contrary to the principles of the majority of our people. They question many of our institutions, includ-ing our economic system. They crusade for radical changes in our system of corporate ownership, changes so drastic that they would all but destroy free enterprise as we know it. Deliberately or not, they are also weak-ening our free competitive system.

Many observers have noted the recent growth of a group of critics who have launched, and have pressed, an assault on the reputation of America. It has already diminished the idea of America in the eyes of many people, at home and abroad. The damage they do is greatest among our young, who are no longer even given the time to judge our system by their own experience. Instead, their ideals are aborted, at an age and often in a place — in our schools — where ideals ought to be instilled rather than destroyed.

The current disparagement of America holds many ironies. One is that the country is criticized for the relatively narrow area of shortcoming without credit for the broad range of achievement. For example, the nation is credited less with a superior system of public higher education than it is criticized for not making it freely available to all, even the unqualified. The nation is credited less with an incomparable transportation system than it is faulted for its traffic jams. The nation is credited less with having two-thirds of its families own their own homes than it is condemned for its slums.

Another irony is that many of today's problems are an outgrowth of yesterday's progress. They are marks of a society that, on the whole, has had extraordinary success in meeting the aspirations of earlier generations. Yet some who criticize our system would substitute other systems which have fallen far short of ours. In most other countries, the quality of our daily life is still no more than a hopeful vision. In those places, such criticisms as we hear would be mere frivolities, idle pastimes of the academic. Where there are no roofs, there are no leaks.

Nevertheless, in our country this climate of disparagement and doubt is real. Its depressing impact upon the national mood is affecting the attitudes and values of our younger generation. All of us with a concern for our society's future must recognize and deal with what is really a kind of national malaise.

To the extent that doubt and disparagement are directed toward free enterprise, they are of direct and immediate concern to us as businessmen. And it is all too evident that, in too many cases, the climate of criticism is highly adverse to free enterprise. The equating of profit with immorality is spreading a cloud of suspicion and distrust over all we have achieved and hope to achieve.

INTELLECTUAL ELITISTS
AND
ECONOMIC FREEDOM

Controlling much of American thought today are intellectual elitists — professors, journalists, artists, bureaucrats. They tend to live in philosophical or abstract worlds, far removed from the ordinary citizen whose main concern is earning a living. And too often, the intellectual looks down upon those from the productive sector. He is surprised, even alarmed, when surveys show that most citizens are not particularly concerned about protecting the right to violent dissent, or the value of unregulated creativity, or the freedom to publish pornography.

And the intellectual elites become suddenly silent when a far more fundamental American freedom is threatened — economic freedom. They never fight for relief from government control of the pocketbook. They fail to realize that economic freedom — the right to hold property and dispose of it under the law, the right to provide security for yourself, your family and your heirs, the right to earn a living untrammeled by economic restraints and social manipulation — is fundamental to a free society. It is the very basis for individual liberty.

Jesse Helms, U.S. Republican Senator from North Carolina.

To those of us in business, progress is both our goal and our habit. We understand that progress means change. We never expect nor want things to stay as they are, much less to turn back to simpler days. Progressive change has brought our country to its present high position. Competitive enterprise has been a principal engine of change and progress. Business has not only responded to change, but has caused change. Out of this process of competitive innovation comes progress.....

The Critics of Business

Many of those who seek change do not share the businessman's obligation to progress. Their goal and their habit is to criticize. They thrive on the sensational accusation and the publicity it gains. At a time when our system is so challenged, all of us — not just some of us — should work to improve free enterprise. None of us can afford to impair it.

This is not to say that any institution in our society should be above criticism, nor that there is no need for criticism. But criticism should be constructive, and doubt should be honest. Doubt truly is the beginning of wisdom, and if the freedom to dissent cannot survive in America, then it can survive no place at all.

Some of today's disparagers, however, lay a false claim to following the noble American tradition of out-spoken criticism. This criticism, however, was for the most part constructive. At heart, these earlier men and women were builders. They were doers, as well as doubters.

Yet too many today seek less to correct a wrong than to condemn a system. Too many critics focus on a particular fault for no more than a moment, and offer few if any solutions. They jump from cause to cause, going wherever popularity or expediency lead, using whatever means are at hand, inflaming any issue that promises attention....

Much of the modern criticism of free enterprise is by no means idle, nor is it intended to be. Many of the critics have the professed aim to alter "the role and influence of corporations and corporate management in and upon American society." Their philosophy is antagonistic to our American ideas of private property and individual responsibility. Henry G. Manne is Kenan Professor of Law and Political Science at the University of Rochester. He has observed that these critics would like to carry corporate decisions into the streets, where they have already taken many of the decisions of some universities and other institutions.

Those critics whose aim is destructive are following a basic tactic of divisiveness — and with considerable success. They are endeavoring to turn various segments of our society — government, labor, the universities — against business. They are trying to make America in the 1970's a society at war with itself.

Their ultimate aim is to alienate the American consumer from business, to tear down long-established relationships which have served both so well. They tell the consumer he is being victimized. New products are being foisted upon him, whether he wants them or not. These products are not as good as they should be — that is, they are less than perfect. Businessmen are greedy and uncaring. Corporations are beyond reach and above response to the consumer's needs. Advertising is false. Prices are padded. Labels are inaccurate. Therefore, the consumer, many would have us believe, is helpless and unprotected when he shops, and is really not responsible for what he buys.

> **The equating of profit with immorality is spreading a cloud of suspicion and distrust over all we have achieved and hope to achieve.**

This delusion — that the consumer cannot trust his own free choice — strikes at the very heart of our free competitive system. The system is founded on the conviction that in the long run the consumer is the best judge of his own welfare. The entire success of free enterprise can be traced to the vitality it gains by competitive striving to satisfy the discriminating customer. To destroy the concept of consumer supremacy is to destroy free enterprise. If the consumer can be convinced that he really does not know what is good for him — and this is what the critics try to do — then freedom leaves free enterprise....

The Social Responsibility of Business

Corporate responsibility is a catchword of the adversary culture that is so evident today. If something is wrong with American society, blame business.

Business did not create discrimination in America, but business is expected to eliminate it. Business did not bring about the deterioration of our cities, but business is expected to rebuild them. Business did not create poverty and hunger in our land, but business is expected to eliminate them....

The climate of criticism and disparagement has dulled the reputation of business. We read and hear very little that is good about business. Seldom, if ever, is business credited with meeting its basic corporate responsibilities. I submit that American business is fulfilling vital social responsibilities every day — and with great success.

Business does its job when it provides useful jobs at high wages, when it provides useful products at fair prices, when it provides economic growth that produces taxes for government and earnings for stockholders. These are the long-standing social responsibilities of business. Their fulfillment by American business over two centuries has made our America what it is. It is an achievement to be proud of — an achievement to talk about....

Business has high goals, large responsibilities, and every incentive to fulfill them. In a climate of under-standing, it can continue to provide rising standards of well-being for ourselves and our families. In a climate of encouragement, business can continue to expand job opportunities for the millions of new workers who are entering the labor force. In a climate of confidence, business can continue to offer the wide variety of quality products which consumers demand. In a climate of growth, business can continue to generate the earnings and pay the dividends on which investors, large and small, depend.

This competitive system of ours has achieved results beyond man's imagining. Its potential for further advance is greater than even the achievements in the past. It is time to tell this story with the enthusiasm and strength to match our conviction.

CAPITALISM IS DESTROYING AMERICA

Tom Christoffel, David Finkelhor, Dan Gilbarg

The following reading is taken from the book, **Up Against the American Myth**. The book is the result of a course offered at Harvard University during the school year of 1968-69. Three graduate students, whose names appear above, organized the course. They wish to argue with those who enrolled "that meaningful social improvement is impossible in this country without the destruction of capitalism, and furthermore, that such a goal is achievable."

Reflect on the following questions while you read:

1. What serious claim do the authors make?
2. Why do the authors claim that the annual growth of the gross national product is not a true indicator of improvement in American society?
3. How do militarism and the automobile negatively affect American society?
4. The authors' final claim is that "ours is a society that does not give priority to people and their needs, but to profit." Do you agree?

Tom Christoffel, David Finkelhor and Dan Gilbarg, **Up Against the American Myth** (Holt, Rinehart and Winston: 1970), pp. 7-18. From **Up Against the American Myth** written and edited by Tom Christoffel, David Finkelhor, Dan Gilbarg. Copyright © 1970 by Tom Christoffel, David Finkelhor and Dan Gilbarg. Reprinted by permission of Holt, Rinehart and Winston, Publishers.

The system of U.S. capitalism is in inevitable, fundamental conflict with the needs of the people who live under its rule. To satisfy those needs, capitalism must be destroyed....

Power resides in the hands of the largest American corporations; this power is used to make profits and to promote the self-interest of these corporations and the small class of people who own, direct and manage them — and finally, that unfettered use of this power is responsible for the persistent inequality in America, for the failure to meet most people's basic material needs, for the proliferation of waste in the form of military weaponry and useless consumer goods and for the insurmountable roadblocks placed in the way of serious social reform....

Income Distribution

The income structure in America has remained virtually static since 1910....While everyone may be getting more, the same *proportion* of income is going to the same income tenths then as now.

This finding has profound implications. It means that in spite of the deep economic and social changes of the last sixty years, those on top continue to appropriate the same lion's share of the pie. This testifies to the entrenched nature of the institutional forces maintaining this structure. It is good a priori evidence that those on top will in the future keep getting the disproportionate share they have gotten in the past. It also suggests that any changes in this allocation are going to require really massive changes in power relations.

THE ENEMY WITHIN

The real threat to "the free-enterprise system" does not come from "radicals, extremists and Marxists," some of whom make too much money as FBI informers to desire seriously the fall of the status quo. The danger to capitalism — the true "enemy within" — is capitalism itself; more precisely, capitalism that says anything goes and allows an excess of provocative extremities no system can long abide.

Bill Moyers, "The Enemy Within," **Newsweek**, June 16, 1975, p. 84.

Economic Concentration

But while the income structure has remained static, there is good reason to believe that, in back of this screen, those on top have been consolidating their power and resources. Real power in the economy lies not so much in individuals as in corporations. And the corporate economy is growing more concentrated year by year. In 1941 the top one thousand corporations controlled two thirds of all manufacturing assets. Today this same two thirds is controlled by a mere two hundred corporations. Real control is passing into fewer and fewer hands. The big corporations using their market leverage...are growing bigger. The conglomerate movement results in the marriages of a number of these giants to create bigger giants with more capital, more market power and more political leverage. Surely this increasing concentration of economic decisions cannot be passed off as a democratization of the society.

The most prominent trend in society is thus not the growth of the middle class, but the growth and consolidation of corporate power.

Affluence

Although real income has increased substantially, doubling over the last twenty years, there are good grounds for questioning whether the lot of the average American has truly improved. Today the average American is buying products he could never before have purchased. But a substantial portion of his increased earnings is being gobbled up by the superfluous and wasteful aspects of those products. He is paying for an enormous proliferation of frills, accessories, advertising needed to sell the product and engineering designed to make it outmoded....

In many ways, the more advanced our society becomes the more expensive is a bare minimum existence. To purchase toothpaste, a poor man has to pay for the "extra-added-ingredients" and the costs of advertising all pegged for the man of "affluence."...

Pattern Of Development: Waste and Neglect

Every year, America's national product gets larger.

To look at the growth of the American economy over the years, it seems like a great success story. But we have to look underneath the statistics about more and more production to understand who has reaped the benefits of this increased production, and of what this production has actually consisted.

To begin with, we know that despite the growth in production, the American economy has failed miserably in the provision of collective goods and services. Mass transportation, medical care, education, housing, child care, recreation — all of these have been seriously neglected, much more than in other capitalist countries of Western Europe and far more than in the Socialist countries. Thus even increases in real income have not been able to satisfy those needs which require not simply consumer goods, but also collective facilities and action by public authorities.

Second, U.S. economic development has not taken place democratically. It has been directed by the corporate managers of America — out of control of the masses of people....

Finally...the *pattern* or *model* of development of the U.S. economy has been one founded on a high-level of military spending, on the one hand, and a huge amount of waste in the production of consumer goods, on the other. To put it another way — if we look at what our ever-increasing production has actually consisted of, we will see that billions represented military goods of all sorts that no one could use. In addition, we have paid in our purchases of consumer goods like automobiles not only for a product that could be used, but for the advertising and market research that went into selling it, for the research and style changes that went into making it look new and different, and for the repairs and the necessity to buy a new product when this one falls apart that comes from the systematic effort of producers to build obsolescence and a short life-span right into their product.

The consequences of this pattern of development — concentration on military spending and the prolifera-tion of consumer waste — are felt not only in our pocketbooks. They have had clear effects on our culture and the prospects of human survival. Let's now try to see the roots of this pattern in the structure of our economy.

FREE ENTERPRISE NO LONGER EXISTS IN AMERICA

The corporate chieftains tell us that in America anyone can save up his income, invest in capital, and become his own boss if he so chooses. What they don't tell us is that while they are busy praising the free enterprise system on the one hand, they have done everything in their power to destroy the competitive market on the other. Take a look at the record. In 1780, over 80 percent of the American people were self-employed. Today, only 10 percent are self-employed, as hundreds of thousands of small businesses have been driven out of the marketplace by a handful of giant conglomerates.... Free enterprise no longer exists in America.

The Peoples Bicentennial Commission, **Common Sense II**, (New York: Bantam Books, Inc. 1975), pp. 20-21.

Militarism

Militarism looks easy to isolate: our society is presently spending $80 billion or close to 10 percent of the vaunted GNP on arms and related expenditures....

This incredible military complex constitutes the most advanced and rapidly developing sector of the economy. Electronics, aerodynamics and telecommunications are the pride and joy of American industry. The vast majority of the nation's research efforts plus the vast majority of the nation's newly trained scientists and engineers are poured into this sector at ever-increasing rates.

And with what result? A showy space program promising little for human betterment and wasting enormous resources for the sake basically of international propaganda. A growing arsenal of weapons many of which are never completed anyway. Aggressive military ventures all over the world. An empire we are obliged to protect, etc. How is this to be accounted for?

A certain portion of defense spending can be attributed to the problem of national defense. That, in less mystified lingo means protecting the world-wide American empire. Real threats to the people of this country are pretty few, except for nuclear annihilation — defense against which is clearly now *not* obtainable through increased armaments. But — as the wasteful way in which it is spent shows — there is an awful lot more behind defense spending than just defense.

Stagnation

Capitalism since its infancy has been plagued by the problem of stagnation. Demand tends to grow less rapidly than production. The market economy — unplanned and uncontrolled — heads into a tail spin — depression, unemployment and falling profits.

But in the wake of the last great economic crisis the system stumbled into a partial remedy. Massive state expenditures for rapidly disposable, expensive items like military weapons could maintain a fairly high level of demand over fairly long periods. What the New Deal was incapable of achieving in terms of bringing the capitalist economy back to life, World War II achieved. The result is the permanent war economy that continues to this very day.

A permanent military sector proved an ideal source of state-stimulated economic demand. (1) It provided virtually limitless projects which quickly became obsolete and required replacement. (2) It was bolstered by a tailor-made ideology — the Cold War. (3) State-financed defense, unlike, say, state-financed housing, in no way competed with the activities of private corporations who would oppose its expansion. These were advantages shared by no other type of possible government expenditure, like public housing or welfare spending. All in all, it spelled an immensely profitable opportunity for a vast array of corporations.

The military establishment is now a permanent feature of the capitalist landscape. It serves a crucial "safety valve" function to the boom-and-bust economy. And in addition, it is enormously profitable. So by now the most powerful corporations in the economy have tied their well-being and prosperity into it, by buying defense corporations and taking on government contract work.

America's international empire also has roots that trace to the heart of the economic system. In part, it too emerged as a response to the same problem of inadequate domestic demand. Corporations have found that markets abroad can be used to absorb goods unused by domestic demand. In addition, the international empire allows our corporations to dominate the world reservoirs of minerals and raw materials. This is the key to maintaining rates of profit far beyond that obtained in most domestic investment. Finally, sending plants overseas to cheap labor supplies can be a way of making big profits and of forcing wage levels down at home. Thus American corporate giants have staked out their claims all over the world. In order to protect this vast complex of economic interests, our political leaders must adopt a massive military arsenal and an aggressive posture toward popular and nationalist movements around the world.

Together, these two overlapping corporate interest groups — militarism and imperialism — are powerful forces behind the priority our system gives to a "garrison economy," as one writer put it. They lobby for it, they profit from it, they are prepared to defend it.

Exorcising this Leviathan is not like operating on a wart — some external excrescence. Since the vested interest in militarism has its roots in the heart of the economy, in the hundred or so largest corporations, eliminating the Military-Industrial Complex means fundamentally changing capitalism. In our view, these corporations cannot be satisfied by some nonmilitary spending substitute. The possibility for enormous profits there is too slim, the cost of changeover is too great. Those who think we can dismantle the MIC without a revolution have serious illusions about where power lies in America.

Consumerism

The model of development characterizing the nonmilitary part of the domestic economy is best described as consumerism. That means a commodity system based on the sale of products to a mass of private individuals for the purposes of individual consumption.

An economy based on consumption that seemed quite normal in a time of scarcity is coming to mean something quite irrational in an era of abundance. The market for consumer goods is now characterized by the sale of more and more useless items. Those items that are still necessary are more and more laden with useless accessories, fringes, decoration and anything that can be used to increase the price. Thousands of virtually identical products — produced with enormous waste in duplication — compete for consumers' attention in supermarkets and department stores under different brand names. To make the system work, billions are spent on advertising to assure a customer's preference for one identical product over another. To increase the general level of consumption, advertising is used to manipulate consumers to be aware of needs and desires they previously had never recognized. This is combined with intentional efforts to reduce the quality of goods, plan early obsolescence in order to obtain a quicker turn-over and repurchase of items. Vast quantities of technology and brain power go into the production of useless values and thinking up marketing schemes.

Here are the results: technological know-how that could be improving existence is wasted on uselessness. Productive capacity is squandered in duplication and needless variation. Human values are debased because people are goaded into placing market prices on everything, on consuming compulsively. Human relationships and aspirations all become associated with commodities, as people are told that buying a car or using a beauty product will make them loved, or give them an identity. The basis for cooperation and trust and openness in the society is undermined, as the most powerful economic institutions in the world manipulate people for profit, and this leaves them feeling exploited, bewildered and suspicious.

Profit

Such an organized system of misrepresentation and manipulation could only grow out of a production-for-profit economy. Companies plan obsolescence, manipulate consumers and market uselessness because it is enormously profitable to do so. It is cheaper than increasing the quality of their products, searching out new consumer needs to satisfy and helping consumers to rationally buy what they need. Under the constraints of competitive capitalism in the old days, companies had incentive to be constructive in these ways. But under monopoly conditions, with many basic commodity needs already satisfied and given the arsenal of manipulative techniques available, the real pathology of capitalism becomes apparent: production is not geared to satisfy needs, but to make money. The two do not coincide....

The Civilization of the Automobile

The automobile is the item of individual consumption par excellence. The average American is encouraged to express himself through the automobile. With it he can compensate for status anxieties; express his manliness; participate in America. Meanwhile, the automobile threatens to destroy our civilization. It makes cities unlivable; it pollutes the air; it spawns a network of congested highways tearing down everything in its path; it creates traffic jams that only intensify the anxiety and irritability acquired on the job; it causes thousands of deaths and millions of injuries per year; its economic costs include billions on highway building and billions on insurance policies.

Real questions are raised about whether it actually improves our quality of life. Congestion and parking mean that cars hardly make it any easier to get to work; a second car for many working-class families is an economic burden not a luxury — papa needs it to get a job, to which he drives the car everyday, only to leave it unused in the company parking lot. Meanwhile, families shell out an enormous amount on repairs, insurance, gas and the inevitable new car required by obsolescence.

No one questions that for an equivalent social expenditure we could build a fantastic system of rapid and low-cost public transportation within cities and between them. Many schemes of local car rentals or car pools have been devised, so that families could have cars for their use when public facilities did not suffice.

But the present system with all its waste is nonetheless enormously profitable, and the corporate interests that stand behind it sport a more enormous range of powers than capitalism has ever seen. What would the automobile companies do without *planned obsolescence* that enables them to furnish an average American with a new car every two and a quarter years? Or the oil interests? Or the construction companies with their cornucopia of fat-filled road-building contracts furnished them by public authorities? Or the rubber and plate-glass interests? Or last but not least, the multibillion dollar insurance companies. It is not surprising that the American public cannot even formulate the idea of an alternative transportation system.

In conclusion, ours is a society that does not give priority to people and their needs, but to profit.

GOVERNMENT REGULATIONS ARE DESTROYING CAPITALISM

Hans F. Sennholz

Dr. Sennholz is Head of the Department of Economics, Grove City College, Pennsylvania. The following reading is taken from **The Freeman**, a monthly journal published by The Foundation for Economc Education. See page 81, at the beginning of Reading 9 for a description of the Foundation.

Think about the following questions while you read:

1. The author believes that fewer government regulations would permit monopolies to develop. Why does he think this would be a good idea?
2. Why does the author believe that effective competition would exist in a monopolistic system?
3. How would the authors of reading seven react to this reading?

Hans F. Sennholz, "The Phantom Called 'Monopoly'," **The Freeman**, March 1960. Reprinted with permission.

In their denunciation of capitalism the socialists use some frightful phantoms. The oldest and perhaps the most effective one is the notion that monopolistic concentration of business inheres permanently and inseparably in capitalism. They depict in vivid colors the horrors of monopolistic capitalism and then conclude that a free enterprise economy obviously requires governmental restraint lest it deteriorate to a chaotic system of business monopolies and public oppression.

Recalling the era of "trust" and "tycoons" around the turn of this century, these socialists valiantly defend the Sherman Antitrust Act of 1890, the Federal Trade Commission Act, and the Clayton Antitrust Act of 1914 which aim at the suppression of business monopoly. And they will be shocked if anyone casts doubt on the wisdom of the antitrust legislation....

An unbiased investigation of the monopoly problem might well begin with the question: Are monopolies inherently bad? Are they identical with destruction of competition, with enormous monopolistic gains, and with gouging of workers and consumers? Under what conditions, if any, are monopolies really the evil organizations which they are assumed to be?

In an unhampered market economy a monopoly affords no cause for alarm. A company that has exclusive control of a commodity or service in a particular market is prevented from exploiting the situation by the following competitive factors: potential competition, competition of substitutes, and the elasticity of demand.

Potential Competition

In the United States thousands of different commodities are each produced by a single producer, i.e., by a monopolist, and no one seems to care about it. The 5 and 10 cent stores are full of items produced by monopolists. And yet, all these items are sold at competitive prices. Why? Because of potential competition. As long as there is potential competition, a monopolist cannot charge monopolistic prices.

Potential competition exists in all fields of production and commerce which anyone is free to enter. In other words, wherever government does not prevent free entry through licenses, franchises, and other controls, potential competition exists. Most corporations are searching continuously for new lines and items of production. They are eager to invade any field in which business earnings are unusually high.

The invasion of another field of a corporation may involve no more than a simple retooling or reorganization that is achieved in a few weeks or months. Or, brand new facilities may be employed for an invasion. Thus one producer, whether he is a monopolist, duopolist, or a competitor among many, always faces the potential competition of all other producers....

Dreading the promoter who may invade his field, the monopolist therefore must act as if he were surrounded by numerous competitors. He must be alert and always "competitive." He must continuously improve his product and reduce its price. For if he should relax, another company will soon invade his field. The newcomer is likely to be a formidable competitor for he has new machinery and equipment. He has new ideas and applies new methods of production. And he enjoys the good will of all customers. Indeed, a monopolist who relaxes invites disaster.

If an enterprise nevertheless enjoys a monopolistic position, it must by necessity be the most efficient producer in the field. In other words, *in an industry endowed with freedom of entrance, a monopoly is an efficiency monopoly.* For the government to impose restrictions on it or even dissolve it by force would be to destroy the most efficient producer and invite the less efficient to enter the field. In this case, the economy suffers a net loss in output and efficiency.

In my hometown a small manufacturer succeeded in gaining a monopolistic position in the production of creep testers, which are machines that test the behavior of materials at elevated temperatures. When I inquired into the reasons for his astonishing position, he explained with a smile: "I completely routed my two competitors, both billion-dollar corporations, by continuously improving the quality of my product and reducing its price. They finally abandoned the field."...

CAPITALISM, U.S.A., TODAY

I wish to submit here a third point of view in a fascinating debate which has recently opened about the nature of the present danger to the capitalist system in the United States....

I would like to submit that there are two trends in the U.S. today which are likely to do more harm to the system than any "plans to socialize America"...

One of these is the tendency of big business and industry to run to government for help when in difficulty. Every time the federal government bails out an ailing corporation it is departing from the concept of a free competitive enterprise. The very essence of capitalism is self-reliance in a competitive condition. Capitalism is at its most efficient when the weak and inefficient and obsolete go to the wall, not to Washington. The company which goes to Washington for a loan is already halfway from enterprise capitalism to nationalized industry.

The second trend is the tendency of the labor unions to demand that government do whatever may be necessary to maintain what is called "full employment." In free-enterprise capitalism, labor is as competitive as business or industry. The individual workingman is in an open and competitive labor market. His job is not guaranteed. The more efficient workers get the better jobs. The others do less well.

The American economy is dominated today by price fixing by big business and wage fixing by big unions. Price and wage fixing would be impossible in a truly free enterprise capitalism. It is inaccurate to call what exists in the U.S. today capitalism. The American system has some competitiveness left in it, but not enough to qualify it as competitive enterprise under Adam Smith definitions.

Joseph C. Harsh, "Capitalism, U.S.A., 1975," **Christian Science Monitor**, June 17, 1975. Reprinted by permission from **The Christian Science Monitor** © 1975 The Christian Science Publishing Society. All rights reserved.

Competition of Substitutes

But even if American enterprises failed to compete with each other and potential competition failed to exert a restraining influence on monopolists — which is a most unrealistic assumption — the people would escape monopolistic pricing through recourse to substitutes. In many fields the competition of substitutes is more important than that of competing producers.

People's wants may be satisfied by a variety of products and materials. In the manufacture of clothing, for instance, a dozen different materials vie with each other for the consumer's dollar. The monopolist of any one material is powerless because monopolistic pricing would induce consumers to switch immediately to other materials....

Demand Elasticity

The existence of substitutes makes for demand elasticity which, in turn, makes monopolistic pricing unprofitable; for higher product prices would greatly curtail product demand, and thus sales and income, of the monopolist. Therefore, he again must act as if he were a competitor among many.

The same is true in all cases of demand elasticity, whether or not there are substitutes. For instance, electricity for heating must compete with such substitutes as oil, gas, and coal. However, as a source of light and of energy for power tools, it probably faces no substitutes. An electricity monopolist, nevertheless, would be greatly restrained by potential competition and demand elasticity.

If electricity prices would rise considerably, the most important consumers, such as industrial plants and other business organizations, would soon produce their own electricity. With the proper equipment anyone can produce his own. Of course, the monopolist may counteract this danger by charging different rates to his different classes of customers: low rates to all industrial users who are apt to produce their own electricity, and higher rates to all others. Assuming that residential users do not readily resort to independent power production, are they not liable to fall in the grip of a monopolist? No! Demand elasticity would prevent this.

Many people undoubtedly could reduce their consumption of electricity without suffering mentionable discomfort. A house owner who may enjoy the light of a hundred bulbs on a winter evening might easily curtail his consumption if electricity charges should increase greatly. But this curtailment of demand would reduce the sales and income of the monopolist.

All producers in fact compete with all other producers for the consumer's dollars. The manufacturer of television sets competes with the manufacturer of freezers and refrigerators. If the monopolist of one commodity — say, television sets — should raise his price, the consumer may forego the purchase of a new set and buy instead a new refrigerator. We consumers do not allocate our income to the satisfaction of categories of wants but to that of specific wants yielding the greatest net addition to our well-being. This addition, in turn, is determined by the urgency of our wants and by the cost of acquisition. Rising costs obviously affect us adversely, which may induce us to purchase an entirely different product that now contributes to our well-being....

An Optimum Growth

In a system of unhampered economic freedom, a monopolistic market position could be attained only through efficiency. Without government intervention, an efficient enterprise tends to grow until it reaches its optimum size at which the unit costs of production are lowest. This optimum depends on the nature of the industry, the state of the product and capital markets, the rate of taxation, and the caliber of management....

There is no need for government to break up a giant enterprise; if it were too large, the competitors would reduce it.

This is not to deny that even in a capitalist economy a monopoly may temporarily reduce output and charge monopolistic prices. Having reached a monopolistic position through efficiency, a businessman may attempt henceforth to follow monopolistic policies. But the foregoing analysis clearly indicates that his attempts are bound to be short-lived. Soon, he will face a crucial struggle with powerful invaders producing with new equipment and enjoying the good will of the public....

It cannot be denied that in our interventionist world many monopolies actually have the power to restrict output and charge monopolistic prices. But the reason for this unfortunate state of affairs is to be found in the multiplicity of government restrictions of competition. If the government prevents competitors from entering the field, the people lose their protection by potential competition. The public utility that enjoys an exclusive franchise is a local monopoly. In this case, the people's only line of resistance is their demand elasticity and perhaps, also, their recourse to independent production. Meanwhile, the planners resort to political controls.

Through franchises, licenses, patents, tariffs, and other restrictions, modern government has in fact created thousands of monopolies. Having thus crippled and hampered competition, it then proceeds to control the monopolies. Political bodies now decide vital economic questions in many important industries. They regulate our railroads, airlines, and other means of transportation. They grant exclusive franchises in radio, television, telephone, and telegraph. They monopolize the production and marketing of electricity, water, and gas. They issue patents that assure their recipients monopolistic positions. And, finally, they own and operate the whole postal industry and prevent competition through fines and imprisonments. In all these cases, the government effectively restricts competition and thus creates local or national monopolies.

CASE STUDY: ECONOMIC DEMOCRACY

Acme Manufacturing Company is a prosperous firm with fine potential for the future. The owner of Acme has offered to sell the company to the one hundred employees who work there. A group of employees is in favor of the purchase and recommends that all employees contribute equally to the purchase price. The group suggests that the employees own and operate the company according to the plan for **Economic Democracy** proposed by the Peoples Bicentennial Commission (see the next page). A copy of the plan is given to each employee to study.

Instructions

STEP 1. The class should break into groups of four to six students.

STEP 2. Each group should pretend that it represents an advisory council appointed by the employees to study the owner's offer and the plan for **Economic Democracy**. The advisory council must recommend whether or not it considers it practical for the employees to buy Acme and run it according to the plan for **Economic Democracy**.

STEP 3. After a majority of the members of each small group has made its decision, it should be able to present its recommendation and reasoning to the whole class.

WE ADVOCATE A NEW ECONOMIC SYSTEM
ECONOMIC DEMOCRACY
— It's neither Capitalism nor Socialism —

Most of us are familiar with Capitalism and Socialism, the two dominant economic systems in the world today. There is, however, a third economic system that is being discussed and experimented with in countries throughout the world. It is a system of self-managed enterprises that operate within a competitive free market economy.

The 5 Defining Characteristics of a "Democratic Economy"

1.) A democratic economy is composed of firms controlled and managed by the people who work in them. Employees determine broad company policies and elect management on the principle of one person one vote.

2.) In a self-managed firm, all participants share in the net income of the enterprise. The members themselves jointly determine the various income levels for different job tasks in the firm.

The members also jointly determine the amount of undistributed net income that will be used for other purposes, such as investment in new capital and reserve funds.

3.) In a democratic economy, the ownership of the capital assets can take one of two forms. Either the working members of that firm directly own the enterprise; or they 'lease' the plant, equipment and other capital assets from an agency of the local or national government, and pay a contractual fee, rental or interest out of the income they generate from the enterprise.

In the latter case, the members of a self-managed firm cannot sell these borrowed assets and distribute the proceeds as current income to the members. The assets are merely being leased and when and if a particular firm decides to go out of business, the capital assets go back to the leasing source. On the other hand, the lenders of financial capital have no right of control over the policies or physical assets of the self-managed firm as long as it is meeting its debt-servicing obligations.

4.) A self-managed system always operates in a competitive free market economy. Firms are free to vie with each other in terms of prices, product quality, and types of products and services in the marketplace.

Economic planning and policy may be exercised by the local or National Government through the use of indirect policy instruments, such as special tax incentives, but never through direct orders or interventions.

Natural resources, utilities and public transportation remain outside the free market economy and are publicly owned and administered in a democratic economy.

5.) In a democratic economy, there is complete freedom of employment. The individual is free to take or not take a job or to leave a particular job.

What is the motivating force of a self-managed economy?

The financial objective of the self-managed firm is to maximize the income of each of its members.

The social objective is to maximize democratic participation of each of its members.

Peoples Bicentennial Commission, Washington, D.C. 20036

3 CHAPTER

AMERICAN POLITICAL VALUES

Readings
9. **Individual Responsibility and Freedom**
   Dean Russell
10. **The New Aristocracy**
    Sidney Lens
11. **Beliefs and Principles of the John Birch Society**
    John H. Rousselot
12. **Our Unspoken National Faith**
    Daniel J. Boorstin

INDIVIDUAL RESPONSIBILITY AND FREEDOM

Dean Russell

Dean Russell wrote this article as a member of the staff of the Foundation for Economic Education. FEE explains its purpose as follows: "State interventionism — popularly called socialism, communism, Fabianism, Nazism, the welfare state, the planned economy or whatever — grows rapidly here in the U.S.A. and elsewhere not because this 'progressive' ideology lacks opponents but because there are so few who adequately understand and can competently and attractively explain interventionism's opposite: the free market, private property, limited government philosophy and its moral and spiritual antecedents. Many have forgotten the real reasons for the freedom and the outburst of creative energy that has marked America."

Consider the following questions while reading:

1. Why did our founding fathers distrust government?
2. What new idea did the founders of the American republic use?
3. How are individual freedom and responsibility related?
4. The author claims that we are losing our freedoms because people are giving government more and more responsibilities. Do you agree?

Dean Russell, "The Bill of Rights," an undated pamphlet distributed by the Foundation for Economic Education. Reprinted by permission from the Foundation for Economic Education.

What was the reason — the real reason — that caused those early American patriots to distrust a federal government which they were about to bring into existence? Why did the individual citizens within the various sovereign states demand a bill of rights before ratifying the Constitution? Why did statesmen of the caliber of Washington, Jefferson, Adams, and Franklin wish to severely restrict the authority of the central government and to strictly limit the power of its leaders?

There was a reason, a vital reason — a reason that many present-day Americans have forgotten. A reason that, unless we relearn it, will surely mean the loss of personal freedom and individual liberty for all mankind.

Here is the reason: The power of government is *always* a dangerous weapon in *any* hands.

The founders of our government were students of history as well as statesmen. They knew that, without exception, every government in recorded history had at one time or another turned its power — its police force — against its own citizens, confiscated their property, imprisoned them, enslaved them, and made a mockery of personal dignity.

That was true of every *type* of government known to mankind. That was true regardless of how the government leaders came to power. It was true — then as now — that government leaders *elected by the people* frequently turn out to be the worst enemies of the people who elect them. Hitler was a recent example. He was not the first; he is not likely to be the last.

A New Idea

It was for this reason that the founders of the American republic introduced into that government a completely new idea.

What was this new idea? Was it the regular election of government leaders by the people? As wise a decision as that was, it was not new. The Greeks, among others, had used it.

82

Was it the wide dispersal of the powers of government among federal, state, and local units? An excellent system, but not new. It had already proved of practical value in France and other countries.

Was the American method of governmental "checks and balances" a new idea? It was a well-conceived plan, but it was not completely original with us. The British system of King, House of Lords, and House of Commons once embodied the same principle.

'ETERNAL VIGILANCE IS THE PRICE OF LIBERTY'

LePelley in **The Christian Science Monitor** © 1974 TCSPS

Here is the new idea: For the first time in known history, a written constitution specified that certain institutions and human relations were to be *outside* the authority of government. The government was specifically forbidden to infringe them or to violate them.

Why Government?

This was a revolutionary concept of government! The idea of inalienable rights and individual freedom had never before been incorporated into a national constitution. Never before in history had the people said to the government: "Thou shalt not." Always the government had been able to say to the people: "You may, or you must." Heretofore, government had *granted* certain freedoms and privileges to the people. But the Bill of Rights said, in effect: "We the people are endowed by our Creator with natural rights and freedoms. The *only* reason for our having a government is to protect and defend these rights and freedoms that we already have as individuals. It is sheer folly to believe that government can give us something that already belongs to us."

These free people then listed in their Constitution those specific functions that they wanted government to handle. Then they forbade the government officials to do anything not commanded of them in the Constitution.

But even so, the people were afraid that the elected leaders of the new government might misunderstand the ideals of human dignity, of individual freedom, of the proper functions of government. So, as specific examples of what they meant, the American people added the Bill of Rights to the Constitution. It might better be called a *Bill of Prohibitions* against government. It is filled with such phrases as: "Congress shall make no law...," "...the right of the people...shall not be infringed...," "The right of the people...shall not be violated...."

These personal and individual rights include freedom of worship, free speech and a free press, the right to assemble together, the sanctity of person and home, trial by jury, the right to life, liberty, and the private ownership of property.

Finally, to make absolutely sure that no government official could possible misinterpret his position as servant rather than master, the people added two more blanket restrictions against the federal government. The Bill of Rights specifies that: "The enumeration...of certain rights shall not be construed to deny...others retained by the people." And: "The powers not delegated to the United States by the Constitution...are reserved to the States...or to the people."

Individual Freedom

It was this philosophy of individual freedom and individual responsiblity — reflected in the Bill of Rights — that attracted to this country millions of persons from the government-oppressed peoples of Europe. They came here from every country in the world. They represented every color, every race, and every creed. They were in search of *personal freedom,* not government-guaranteed "security." And as a direct result of the individual freedom specified by the Constitution and the Bill of Rights, they earned the greatest degree of security ever enjoyed by any people anywhere.

Those new Americans swelled the tide of immigrants by writing the praise of freedom in their letters to relatives and friends who still lived in the countries with *strong* governments, with *one-man* rule, with *government ownership* of the means of production, with *government-guaranteed* "security," with *government* housing, and *state-controlled* education.

Equal Rights

Their letters read, in effect: "Here the government guarantees you nothing except life, liberty, and the right to own whatever you have honestly acquired. Here you have the personal responsibility that goes with individual freedom. There is no law or custom that prevents you from rising as high as you are able. You can associate with anyone who wishes to associate with you. Here in America you can do as you please as long as you do not violate the rights of other persons to do as they please. These rights are recorded in the American Constitution and the Bill of Rights. The same documents specify that three-fourths of the states must be in agreement before these rights can be taken away. And, of course, it is foolish to imagine that the people will ever voluntarily give up their freedom."

AMERICAN CHARACTER HAS SOFTENED

The dateline is London, March 22, 1775. The occasion: Edmund Burke's speech on conciliation with the American colonies....

Burke was 46 that spring. He had been re-elected to Commons a few months earlier. As an acknowledged leader of the opposition, he was just growing into those significant powers of thought and speech that would serve him to his death in 1797. It is Burke to whom American conservatives look today as the fountainhead of their philosophy. His insights, like good wine, grow better with the years....

Burke pleaded with the king's ministers to consider both the advantages of peaceful trade and the uncertainties of distant war. But there was a third consideration as to America: "I mean its temper and character."

"In this character of the Americans a love of freedom is the predominating feature which marks and distinguishes the whole... This fierce spirit of liberty is stronger in the English colonies, probably, than in any other people of the earth."...

What has become of that "love of freedom that 200 years ago marked the American character? Is it still strong, still lively? Does our temper still embrace "a fierce spirit of liberty"? The melancholy answer is no. As a people we are less independent, less self-reliant, less passionately dedicated to personal responsibility than we were two centuries ago....

The American character has softened, weakened, grown feeble with age.

James J. Kilpatrick, "In 200 Years America Has Lost Something," **Minneapolis Star**, March 24, 1975. "Copyright Washington Star Syndicate 1975".

Such letters would not be completely true today, because that freedom is gradually being lost. But the "progressive" laws and "popular" court decisions of recent years are not primarily responsible for it. Freedom is seldom lost by a direct vote on the subject. In our case, it just seems to be *seeping* away. The Bill of Rights still exists on paper, but the *spirit* that caused it to be written is disappearing. When that spirit is completely gone, the written words will mean nothing.

Thus it behooves us to inquire why that spirit is now weak, and how it can be revived.

Who Is To Blame?

No one person is responsible for sapping that spirit of individualism. No one political party is to blame. The people are as responsible as the elected and appointed leaders. It is we the people who seem to have forgotten that freedom and responsibility are inseparable. It is we the people who are discarding the concept of government that brought forth the Declaration of Independence, the Constitution, and the Bill of Rights.

In short, few of us seem to want to keep government out of our personal affairs and responsibilities. Many of us seem to favor various types of government-guaranteed and compulsory "security." We *say* that we want personal freedom, but we *demand* government housing, government price controls, government-guaranteed jobs and wages. We *boast* that we are responsible persons, but we *vote* for candidates who promise us special privileges, government pensions, government subsidies, and government electricity.

Such schemes are directly contrary to the spirit of the Bill of Rights. Our heritage is being lost more through weakness than through deliberate design. The Bill of Rights still shines in all its splendor, but many of us are looking in another direction. Many of us are drifting back to that old concept of government that our forefathers feared and rejected. Many of us are now looking to government for security. Many of us are no longer willing to accept individual responsibility for our own welfare. Yet personal freedom cannot exist without individual responsibility.

Your Choice

Thus the American people are on the verge of a final decision. We must choose between the destruction caused by government paternalism, and the security insured by individual freedom with individual responsibilty as expressed in the Bill of Rights. There is no other choice.

THE NEW ARISTOCRACY

Sidney Lens

Mr. Lens, a Chicago based labor leader and activist in peace and radical movements, is the author of a number of books, including, most recently, **The Promise and Pitfalls of Revolution**.

Consider the following questions while reading:

1. Why did the founding fathers fear corporations?
2. What does the author mean when he says ''we have converted the moral justification of laissez-faire capitalism into justification for state-managed capitalism?
3. Why does the author feel that we have a new aristocracy and ''government without the consent of the governed?'' Do you agree?

Sidney Lens, ''The Moral Roots of the New Despair,'' **The Christian Century**, February 26, 1975, pp. 193-96. Copyright 1975 Christian Century Foundation. Reprinted by permission from the February 26, 1975 issue of **The Christian Century**.

Back in 1776, Thomas Jefferson, following Thomas Hobbes and others, framed his famous Declaration of Independence, which boldly stated that government derives its powers from the consent of the governed. The economic and moral underpinning for this thesis was provided by a 53-year-old Scottish professor named Adam Smith, who that same year published his equally famous **Inquiry into the Nature and Causes of the Wealth of Nations**.

Men and women who met on the freemarket to exchange shoes and wheat, Dr. Smith conceded, were motivated by greed, the desire to pay less for what they bought and to receive more for what they sold. But if this motive was a moral minus, it was like the pain inflicted by a dentist who drills into a cavity to preserve the tooth. Out of the individual greed of millions of buyers and sellers, said Dr. Smith, would come a great collective good; for the gladiators who challenged each other on the free market were forced to improve their products, and often lower their prices, in order to defeat their competitors. Hence they unwittingly gave us access to more and better goods, improved our living standards, and assured progress.

In accord with this concept of the free market came other freedoms to supplement and enhance it: the freedom of an individual to engage in enterprise, the freedom to speak his mind and worship his God, the freedom to choose those who govern, as well as protection *from* those who govern, through a system of "checks and balances" whereby each of the three branches of government curbed the power of the others. It was a nice, symmetrical system, deemed morally sound, for while it unleashed individual greed, it also placed all individuals on an equal footing. The *sine qua non* of this free-enterprise system was that the government must not intervene in favor of one person against another, but must let their talents play themselves out in the free market. To further assure a fair contest, the government was expected to prevent the coagulation of economic power into monopoly....

Early capitalism rested on the moral thesis that the person who risked failure and the loss of his savings was entitled to the reward — profits. So insistent were our forebears on this principle that they looked with disdain on the corporate form of business — because it limited the liability, the risk, of the shareholders.

At the Constitutional Convention the delegates rejected a proposal that would give the federal government the right to issue corporate charters, the general view being that corporations were a dangerous institution leading to monopoly and, worse, aristocracy. That right remained with the states, and under very restricted conditions. Long into the 19th century, corporations were circumscribed as to the amount of capital they could solicit ($100,000, for instance, in New York under the law of 1811); they were usually confined to a single type of operation (say, textile manufacturing or flour milling): and they were required to dissolve after a specific number of years, 20 or 30. As of the year 1800, there were only 335 corporations in the U.S., more than two-thirds of them in turnpike, bridge and canal companies, and only six in manufacturing.

A Welfare State for the Rich

Nonetheless, in due course the corporation — an institution that limits individual risk — became the dominant form of business venture. Worse still, since the Great Depression, more and more of that risk has been placed on the shoulders of government. Side by side with the welfare state for the poor (welfare, public service jobs, unemployment compensation, social security, Medicare), there has arisen a welfare state for the rich that is awesome to contemplate.

The keel for this second welfare state, like that for the first, was laid by the New Deal. It began as an emergency measure whereby the government did for business and banking what they were unable to do for themselves....

What started as an emergency action, however, has now become a way of life: the role of government in the economy is infinitely more important than that of the entrepreneur, whether corporate or individual. Government, through the Federal Reserve and its own budget, manipulates the money supply and interest rates, so that in effect its decisions are the decisive factor in capital formation. A few years ago, when the seventh largest corporation in America, Penn Central, was on the verge of forfeiting on hundreds of millions of dollars in short-term loans, the Federal Reserve saved hundreds of banks from bankruptcy — and the

'ASK NOT WHAT YOU CAN DO FOR YOUR COUNTRY — BUT RATHER WHAT YOU CAN DO TO GET VOTES'

economy from catastrophe — by offering to cover all the loans required at that point to maintain stability.

Government is also by far business's biggest customer; it now spends one out of every three or three and a half dollars of the gross national product. Without it the defense industry would collapse overnight, and many others — construction, steel, agriculture, glass, oil, export, rubber, communications, auto, to name a few — would slowly strangle. Government is far and away the major researcher and developer, spending about $18 billion a year for this purpose — most of which ultimately redounds to the benefit of industry. To get some idea of the overriding scope of the government's role in the economy, consider what has happened to taxes: back in 1885, taxes levied by Washington came to $1.98 per person; by 1970, the figure was $960.07 — 500 times higher. In 1902, state and local governments spent $12.80 for each citizen within their confines; in 1970, they spent $646.20 — 50 times higher.

Not a single major American industry could survive today without government. Detroit's automakers build mechanical wonders that glide along at 80 miles an hour; but they would glide nowhere without the $16 billion spent annually by government to maintain and extend the 4 million miles of roads. Once upon a time, in early America, the risk for building turnpikes was assumed by private companies; now it is assumed entirely by the public, which pays for highways through the tax structure.

Public Risk, Private Profit

As a measure of how the risk has been shifted from private entrepreneurs to the public, consult, if you will, a 1965 report of the Joint Economic Committee. It contains ten cramped pages of small type listing the forms of government subsidy that flow to the affluent. Some of it is direct subsidy (e.g., sums paid to shipping firms to keep them competitive with foreign firms); some of it is indirect (e.g., tax credits for investment in new machinery or depletion allowances to the oil and mineral industries); but, according to Jerry Jasinowski of that committee's staff, it totals $63 billion a year.

A few years ago, when the railroads protested that they were losing money on passenger service, the government bailed them out by forming a quasi-public corporation, Amtrak, to "socialize" their losses. For every dollar in risk capital contributed by private companies to manufacture the supersonic transport plane (SST), the government, according to author Leonard Baker, contributed $6.50. The government guarantees hundreds of millions in loans to bankrupt firms such as Penn Central because private banks refuse to take the risk without such guarantees. The Pentagon alone has made 3,500 loans and subsidies to shore up small firms on the verge of disaster. As of two or three years ago, the federal government had outstanding the astronomical sum of $56 billion in direct loans and another $167 billion in loans it had guaranteed, or a total of $223 billion.

This is no longer Adam Smith's capitalism, but what I. F. Stone calls "private socialism" — the public takes much or most of the risk; private entrepreneurs take the whole profit....

The economic issue blends with the moral one — on whose interests shall the government be operated? The dictionary defines morality as that which is "good and right." The moral stance of the nation originally was that the "greatest good for the greatest number" would ensue if the risk-takers — capitalists — were rewarded with profits commensurate with their risks and talents. But while those risks have progressively declined and in some industries (such as defense) are now zero, the rewards to the goliaths of business are immeasurably higher. And by the same token, without public awareness or discussion, we have converted the moral justification for laissez-faire capitalism into justification for state-managed capitalism....

A New Aristocracy

Concurrent with the shift in moral values vis-a-vis the economy, there has been a similar shift vis-a-vis politics. The founders of the nation feared more than anythng else a return to "aristocracy" — to concentrated and monolithic power. Their solution was to arm the individual with certain inalienable guarantees, contained in the Bill of Rights, and to *disarm* the government by constructing a system of checks and balances to ensure that none of the three branches — and in particular the executive — became all-powerful. This was to be the essence of political democracy.

Again, the system never worked in practice as it was blueprinted in theory, in considerable measure because of the deficiency in *economic* democracy. Nonetheless the structure was there. In the past 40 years that structure has been steadily undermined. The enlarging sphere of state management in the economy, paralleled by the emergence of an enormous military-CIA machine that engages in thousands of secret acts not subject to popular perusal, has brought the nation to a new configuration of power, a new type of aristocracy....

ECONOMICS IGNORES EQUALITY

The essential value of our political Constitution is the equality of all individuals — before the law, in access to the franchise, in political organization, in public debate, in the pursuit of happiness. But this value is ignored in the debasing scramble for economic privilege, the determined defense of established interests, and the mirage of happiness in higher and higher levels of personal consumption.

Peter Walshe, ''Reappraising America's Ideology,'' **The National Catholic Reporter**, January 18, 1974.

There is no question that the moral theme of ''government by consent of the governed'' is being converted into its opposite, ''government without consent of the governed.'' In the area of foreign policy we are thrust into wars and involved in dozens of interventions, military and otherwise, into the affairs of foreign nations without the consent of either Congress or the public. No one discussed whether it was right for the CIA to overthrow the governments of Guatemala and Iran, or to help Mobutu against Lumumba, or to preserve the monarchy in Ethiopia, or to ''destabilize'' the Allende government in Chile.

95

There is no public debate on the issue of militarism; not even members of Congress effect policy here — except on trivia. Article 1, Section 8, of the Constitution, which provides that only Congress can declare war, has been violated wholesale, and the provision that only the Senate can ratify treaties has been made all but meaningless by dozens of secret "contingency agreements" with the dictators of Spain, Thailand, Ethiopia, Brazil, Bolivia, etc., without the Senate's concurrence. After World War II the executive branch of government argued that it needed absolute power in foreign affairs because (1) in a nuclear age, when missiles can make the trip from Moscow to New York in 20 minutes, there is no time to consult Congress and the people, and (2) the "secret, subversive" techniques of the communists can be challenged only by subversion and secrecy on our part. Hence the President is entitled to, and for all practical purposes has received, carte blanche....

The Moral Dilemma

There is very little we can do to influence those decisions. The public seems to sense that, because in the 1974 elections only 38 per cent of eligible voters bothered to go to the polls and only 14 per cent were able to name the two candidates running for Congress in their district. So meaningless has the electoral process become that the most persistent activity of the candidates is not to discuss issues but to gain "name recognition."...

Unless we change our moral guidelines...the pendulum of history will swing from freedom to totalitarianism.

BELIEFS AND PRINCIPLES OF THE JOHN BIRCH SOCIETY

John H. Rousselot

Congressman John Rousselot currently represents California's twenty-sixth congressional district in the U.S. House of Representatives. He is the former director of public relations for the John Birch Society and a current member of the Society. He has been active in Republican party activities in California, and once served as president of the Young Republicans of California. He currently serves on House committees on Banking, and Currency, Post Office and Civil Service.

As you read consider the following questions:

1. Why does the John Birch Society prefer a republic to a democracy? Do you agree?
2. Why does the John Birch Society believe in small governmental units?
3. How do you think a John Birch Society member would react to the claims made by Sidney Lens in the previous reading?

Hon. John H. Rousselot, Congressman from California, in the House of Representatives on Tuesday, June 12, 1962.

We believe that a constitutional Republic, such as our Founding Fathers gave us, is probably the best of all forms of government. We believe that a democracy, which they tried hard to obviate, and into which the liberals have been trying for 50 years to convert our Republic, is one of the worst of all forms of government. We call attention to the fact that up to 1928 the U.S. Army Training Manual still gave our men in uniform the following quite accurate definition, which would have been thoroughly approved by the Constitutional Convention that established our Republic. "Democracy: A government of the masses. Authority derived through mass meeting or any form of 'direct' expression, results in mobocracy. Attitude toward property is communistic — negating property rights. Attitude toward law is that the the will of the majority shall regulate, whether it be based upon deliberation or governed by passion, prejudice, and impulse, without restraint or regard to consequences. Results in demagogism, license, agitation, discontent, anarchy." It is because all history proves this to be true that we repeat so emphatically: "This is a Republic, not a democracy; let's keep it that way."

We are opposed to collectivism as a political and economic system, even when it does not have the police-state features of Communism. We are opposed to it no matter whether the collectivism be called socialism or the welfare state or the New Deal or the Fair Deal or the New Frontier, or advanced under some other semantic disguise. And we are opposed to it no matter what may be the framework or form of government under which collectivism is imposed. We believe that increasing the size of government, increasing the centralization of government, and increasing the functions of government all act as brakes on material progress and as destroyers of personal freedom.

We believe that even where the size and functions of government are properly limited, as much of the power and duties of government as possible should be retained in the hands of as small governmental units as possible, as close to the people served by such units as possible. For the tendencies of any governing body to waste, expansion, and despotism all increase with the distance of that body from the people governed; the more closely any governing body can be kept under observation by those who pay its bills and provide its

FIVE REASONS FOR AMERICA'S SUCCESS

Today in our affluent society, we are enjoying so much of the fruits of this great system of ours that most of us forget just how and why we have become so prosperous.

How is it that one-seventeenth of the world's population can produce almost one half of the world's wealth? How could the American people, in the short span of five generations, have changed an undeveloped wilderness continent into the tremendously rich and powerful nation that we now take for granted?

Well, first our Founding Fathers wrote the Constitution, the greatest document to govern people that the world has ever seen. Living and working under our Constitution and Bill of Rights, Americans created the most successful major society in all human history — and they did it all without government aid. It was built on these five principles:

(1) We had a <u>belief in God</u> — and this religious background made us reliable and dependable with one another.
(2) We had <u>limited government</u> — and this limited our national expenses and gave us surplus capital for tools and a good living standard.
(3) We had <u>individual freedom</u> — every man could work at what he wanted.
(4) We had <u>incentive</u> — which was simply the right to keep the fruits of our labor.
(5) We had <u>competition</u> — the thing that makes businessman and employee alike serve his fellow man well.

From "Will We Keep Our Freedom?" by Walter Knott. A pamphlet published by Americanism Educational League.

delegated authority, the more honestly responsible it will be. And the diffusion of governmental power and functions is one of the greatest safeguards against tyranny man has yet devised. For this reason it is extremely important in our case to keep our township, city, county, and state governments from being bribed and coerced into coming under one direct chain of control from Washington.

We believe that for any people eternal vigilance is the price of liberty far more as against the insidious encroachment of internal tyranny than against the danger of subjugation from the outside or from the prospect of any sharp and decisive revolution. In a republic we must constantly seek to elect and to keep in power a government we can trust, manned by people we can trust, maintaining a currency we can trust, and working for purposes we can trust (none of which we have today). We think it is even more important for the government to obey the laws than for the people to do so. But for 30 years we have had a steady stream of governments which increasingly have regarded our laws and even our Constitution as mere pieces of paper, which should not be allowed to stand in the way of what they, in their omniscient benevolence, considered to be "for the greatest good of the greatest number." (Or in their power-seeking plans pretended so to believe.) We want a restoration of a "government of laws, and not of men" in this country; and if a few impeachments are necessary to bring that about, then we are all for the impeachments.

OUR UNSPOKEN NATIONAL FAITH

Daniel J. Boorstin

Daniel J. Boorstin is the Director of The National Museum of History and Technology of the Smithsonian Institution in Washington, D.C. He has authored many book and won several literary prizes. His book, **The Genius of American Politics**, is an elaboration of the reading below.

Use the following questions to assist your reading:

1. What basic paradox does Mr. Boorstin see in American political thinking?
2. What American characteristic does the author refer to in his use of the term ''Givenness?'' What three factors account for this?
3. Why does the author feel that our political parties have no fundamental theoretical differences?
4. What does our choice of national heroes tell us about ourselves?

Daniel J. Boorstin, ''Our Unspoken National Faith,'' **Commentary**, June 12, 1953, pp. 327-36. ''Reprinted from **Commentary**, by permission; Copyright © 1953 by the American Jewish Committee.''

The marvelous success and vitality of American institutions is equaled by the amazing poverty and inarticulateness of our theorizing about politics. No nation has ever believed more firmly that its political life was based on a perfect theory — and yet no nation has ever been less interested in political philosophy, or produced less in the way of a theory. To explain this paradox is to find a key to much that is characteristic — and much that is good — in our way of life....

The essential fact is that we have always been more interested in *how our society works* than we have in its theoretical foundations....

The tendency to abstract the principles of political life may sharpen issues for the political philosopher. It becomes idolatry when it provides statesmen or a people with a blueprint for remaking their society. Especially in our own age (and at least since the French Revolution of 1789), more and more of the world has sought in social theory no mere rationale for institutions, but just a blueprint. The characteristic tyrannies of our age — Nazism, Fascism, and Communism — have expressed precisely this idolatry. They justify their outrages because their ''philosophies'' require them. Recent European politics shows us men of all complexions seeking explicit ideological systems for society....

> **No nation has ever believed more firmly that its political life was based on a perfect theory — and yet no nation has been less interested in political philosophy, or produced less in the way of a theory.**

Givenness and American Values

The American experience is unique, and this dooms to failure any attempt to sum up our way of life in slogans and dogmas. This is why we have nothing in the line of a theory that can be exported to other peoples of the world.

At the heart of the matter lies a characteristically American belief for which I have invented the name "givenness." It is our way of taking for granted that an explicit political theory is superfluous for us precisely because we already somehow possess a satisfactory equivalent. "Givenness" is the belief that values in America are in some way or other automatically defined: *given* by certain facts of geography or history peculiar to us.

This conviction has three faces: first, we believe that we have received our values as a gift from the *past;* that the earliest settlers or Founding Fathers equipped our nation at its birth with a perfect and complete political theory adequate to all our future needs.

The second is the notion that in America we receive values as a gift from the *present;* that our theory is always implicit in our institutions. This is the idea that the American Way of Life harbors an American Way of Thought, which can do us for a political theory, even if we never make it explicit, or never are in a position to confront ourselves with it.

The third part of "givenness" is a belief which links these first two. It is a belief in the *continuity* or homogeneity of our history. We see our national past as an uninterrupted continuum of similar events, so that our past merges indistinguishably into our present. This makes it easy for us to believe, at the same time, in the idea of a pre-formed original theory given to us by the Founding Fathers, and the idea of an implicit theory always offered us by our present experience. Our feeling of continuity in our history makes it easy for us to see the Founding Fathers as our contemporaries. It induces us to draw heavily on the materials of our history, but always in a distinctly non-historical frame of mind.

American Values As A Gift From the Past

The dominating idea that our values are a gift from our past may be likened to the obsolete biological notion of "pre-formation." That is the idea that all parts of an organism pre-exist in perfect miniature in the seed. Biologists used to believe that if you could look at the seed of an apple under a strong enough microscope you would see in it a minute apple tree. Similarly, we seem to believe that if we could understand the ideas of the earliest settlers — the Pilgrim Fathers or Founding Fathers — we would find in them no mere 17th or 18th century philosophy of government, but the perfect embryo of the theory by which we now live. We believe, then, that the mature political ideals of the nation existed clearly conceived in the minds of our patriarchs....

Our belief in a perfectly pre-formed theory helps us understand many things about ourselves. In particular, it helps us to see how it has been that, while we in the United States have been unfertile in political theories we have possessed an overweening sense of political orthodoxy. But in building an orthodoxy from what are in fact quite scanty early materials, we have of necessity left the penumbra of heresy vague. The inarticulate character of American political theory has thus actually facilitated heresy hunts and tended to make them indiscriminate. The heresy hunts which come at periods of national fear — the Alien and Sedition Acts of the age of the French Revolution, the Palmer Raids of the age of the Russian Revolution, and similar activities of more recent times — are directed not so much against acts of espionage, as against acts of irreverence toward that orthodox American creed supposed to have been born with the nation itself....

It is commonplace that no fundamental theoretical difference separates our American political parties. What need has either party for an explicit political theory where both must be spokesmen of the *original* American doctrine on which the nation was founded?...

The mystic rigidity of our ''pre-formation'' theory has not, however, militated against great flexibility in dealing with practical problems. Confident that the wisdom of the Founding Fathers somehow made provision for all future emergencies, we have not felt bound to limit our experiments to those which we could justify with theories in advance. In the last century or so, whenever the citizens of continental Western Europe have found themselves in desperate circumstances, they have had to choose among political parties each of which was committed to a particular theoretical foundation for its whole program — ''monarchist'' — ''liberal'' — ''Catholic'' — ''socialist'' —

AMERICAN POLITICAL VALUES

Out of the heritage from England, the experience with government in the colonies, the struggle for independence, the weakness of the Confederation, the creation of the Federal Republic, and the experience of more than a century and a half of independence, including four years of civil war (1861-1865), have come American values in the area of politics:

1. The concept of the state as a utilitarian device created to provide for the common defense and to further the general welfare.

2. Freedom and responsibility of the individual adult citizen to have a voice in the government under which he lives, as exemplified in the right and responsibility to vote.

3. Freedom of access to knowledge of all kinds save only when disclosure of particular information would endanger the whole community. This access is achieved through a system of public education, the practice of academic freedom, and the existence of a free press.

4. Freedom to express orally or in writing opinions honestly held concerning economic, religious, political, or social matters. In the case of political opinions, this freedom is limited by the requirements that actions to carry opinions into effect must conform to the procedures for changing the policies or structure of the state as set forth in the Constitution of the United States. A further general limitation is that expression of opinion must not be so inciting as to create a clear and present danger of panic or disorder.

5. The protection of the free citizen against unreasonable invasions of privacy by officers of government.

6. The right of free citizens to assemble peaceably.

> 7. The supremacy of civil authority over the military in conformity with the principle that the civil authority is the decision-making power and the military is the instrument, when needed, to carry decisions into effect.
>
> 8. The concept of the American Federation as a "permanent union of permanent states," firmly established after the Civil War, maintained by judicial enforcement of the Constitution and forbidding nullification or secession on the part of the states.

Ralph H. Gabriel, **American Values: Continuity and Change** (Westport, Connecticut: Greenwood Press, 1974), pp. 161-62. Reprinted by permission of the publishers, Greenwood Press, a division of Williamhouse-Regency Inc., 51, Riverside Avenue, Westport, Connecticut, 06880, and the author Ralph H. Gabriel from his **American Values: Continuity and Change**, first published in 1974.

"fascist" — or "Communist." This has not been the case in the United States. Not even during the Civil War: historians still argue over what, if any, political theory Lincoln represented. In the crisis which followed the Great Depression, when Franklin D. Roosevelt announced his program for saving the American economy, he did not promise to implement a theory. Rather he declared frankly that he would try one thing after another and would keep trying until a cure was found....

American Values As A Gift From the Present

We have been told again and again, with the metaphorical precision of poetry, that the United States is the *land* of the free. Independence, equality, and liberty, we like to believe, are breathed in with our very air. No nation has been readier to identify its values with the peculiar conditions of its landscape: we believe in *American* equality, *American* liberty, *American* democracy, or, in sum, the *American* way of life.

Our belief in the mystical power of our land in this roundabout way has nourished a naturalistic point of view; and a naturalistic approach to values has thus, in the United States, been bound up with patriotism itself. What the Europeans have seen as the gift of the past,

Americans have seen as the gift of the present. What the European thinks he must learn from books, museums, and churches, from his culture and its monuments, the American thinks he can get from contemporary life, from seizing peculiarly American opportunities....

The character of our national heroes bears witness to our belief in "givenness," our preference for the man who seizes his God-given opportunities over him who pursues a great private vision. Perhaps never before has there been such a thorough identification of normality and virtue. A "red-blooded" American must be a virtuous American; and nearly all our national heroes have been red-blooded, outdoor types who might have made the varsity team.... Our national heroes have not been erratic geniuses like Michelangelo or Cromwell or Napoleon but rather men like Washington and Jackson and Lincoln, who possessed the commonplace virtues to an extraordinary degree.

The Continuity of American Values

The third aspect of the idea of "givenness" helps us understand how we can at once appeal to the past and the present, and find no contradiction in doing so.

By this I mean the remarkable continuity or homogeneity of American history. To grasp it, we must at the outset discard a European cliche about us, namely that ours is a land without continuity or tradition, while in Europe man feels close to his ancestors. The truth of the matter is that anyone who goes to Europe nowadays cannot fail to be impressed with the amazing, the unique continuity of American history, and, in contrast, the *dis*continuity of European history....

Let me explain. I have recently been abroad, where I spent the better part of a year in Italy. My impressions there sharpened that contrast which I have been describing between the American and the European image of the past. The first church I visited was the Capella Palatina in Palermo, where Christian mosaics of the 12th century are surmounted by a ceiling of Moslem craftsmanship. Throughout Sicily one comes upon pagan temples on the foundations of which rose churches which in the Middle Ages were transformed into mosques, and which later again were used as Christian chapels....

In Europe one need not be an archaeologist or a philosopher to see that over the centuries many different kinds of life are possible in the same place and for the same people. Who can decide which, if any of these, is "normal" for Italy? It is hardly surprising, then, that the people of Europe have not found it easy to believe that their values are given by their landscape. They look to ideology to help them choose among alternatives.

In the United States, of course, we see no Colosseum, no Capella Palatina, no ancient roads. The effect of this simple fact on our aesthetic sense, though much talked of, is probably less significant than on our sense of history and our approach to values. We see very few monuments to the uncertainties, the motley possibilities of history, or for that matter to the rise and fall of grand theories of society. Our main public buildings were erected for much the same purpose for which they are now being used. The Congress of the United States is still housed in the first building expressly constructed for that purpose. Although the White House, like the Capitol, was gutted by fire during the War of 1812, it, too, was soon rebuilt on the same spot; in 1952 another restoration was completed. Our rural landscape, with a few scattered exceptions — the decayed plantation mansions of the South, the manor houses of upstate New York, and the missions of Florida and California — teaches us very little of the fortunes of history....

The impression which the American has as he looks about him is thus one of the inevitability of the particular institutions, the particular kind of society in which he lives.

DISTINGUISHING BETWEEN BIAS AND REASON

The Wizard of Id by permission of John Hart and Field Enterprises, Inc.

Public opinion polls taken after the Watergate scandal show a lack of confidence in elected officials on the part of the American people. The cartoon in this activity exemplifies this skepticism of American politicians.

All Americans have opinions of American political institutions, traditions, and politicians. Some of these opinions are based only on feelings and others are based on facts. One of the most important critical thinking skills is the ability to distinguish between opinions based on emotions or bias and conclusions based on a rational consideration of the facts.

Some of the following statements have been taken from the readings in this book and some have other origins. Consider each statement carefully. Mark **R** for any statement you feel is based on reason and a rational consideration of the facts. Mark **B** for any statement you believe is based on bias, prejudice or emotion. Mark **I** for any statement you think is impossible to judge. Then discuss and compare your judgments with other class members.

R = A STATEMENT BASED ON REASON
B = A STATEMENT BASED ON BIAS
I = A STATEMENT IMPOSSIBLE TO JUDGE

_____ 1. The power of government is always a dangerous weapon in any hands.

_____ 2. The American character has softened, weakened, grown feeble with age.

_____ 3. Today in the United States, it is popular among self-styled "intellectuals" to sneer at patriotism.

_____ 4. There is too much concern in America for the "welfare bum."

_____ 5. We have always been more interested in how our society works than we have in its theoretical foundations.

_____ 6. Basically we are a country of racists.

_____ 7. The most important social contribution that organized religion could make in this country would be to educate people away from the core myth of American individualism.

_____ 8. The Creator made life a competitive game and wherever there is competition there will be those who succeed and those who fail.

_____ 9. Patriotism is the most practical of all human characteristics.

_____10. If it is unpatriotic to tear down the flag (which is a symbol of the country), why isn't it more unpatriotic to desecrate the country itself — to pollute, despoil and ravage the air, land and water?

_____11. These are the three main values — personal freedom, economic well-being, a rich spiritual heritage — and America provides all three of them to the greatest degree ever known in the history of mankind.

111

CHAPTER

AMERICAN
SOCIAL
VALUES

Readings
13. **Cooperation Instead of Competition**
    Ashley Montagu
14. **American Virtues: Individualism and Self-Reliance**
    George W. Maxey
15. **The Values of the Non-Indian World**
    Ed McGaa
16. **Sports Mirror American Values**
    Robert J. Bueter
17. **Our Dominant Cultural Values**
    Cora Dubois

COOPERATION INSTEAD OF COMPETITION

Ashley Montagu

Dr. Ashley Montagu was born and educated in England. He came to the United States in 1927. After receiving his PhD from Columbia, he taught at Harvard and New York universities. From 1949 to 1955 he was chairman of anthropology at Rutgers. He is the author of more than thirty-five books.

Use the following questions to assist your reading:

1. Why does the author prefer emphasis on cooperation rather than competition in America?
2. Why does the author believe it is more efficient to cooperate rather than compete?

Ashley Montagu, **The American Way of Life** (New York: G. P. Putnam's Sons, 1967), page 106-08. Reprinted by permission of G. P. Putnam's Sons from **The American Way of Life** by Ashley Montagu. Copyright © 1952, 1962, 1967 by Ashley Montagu.

At chamber of commerce lunches and on similar occasions one not infrequently hears the orator of the day asserting that "America owes its greatness to the spirit of competition." I would like to suggest that the evidence indicates that whatever greatness America has achieved, it has achieved in spite of competition, *not* because of it. But this is not the main point I wish to make here. My main desire is to clarify the ideas of competition and cooperation as they are actually found to work in an industrial society.

Competition means to strive *against* others to achieve the same or similar goals. Cooperation means to strive *with* others to achieve the same or similar goals. A principle of American way of life is the idea of competition. This takes the simple form of going out and doing better than the other even if you have to do him and his family injury in the process. *That* can be none of your concern. After all, you have *your* family to think of. This kind of indifference to the consequences to others of one's competitiveness is inherent in the principle of competition. Our studies have shown us that this kind of competitiveness is extremely damaging to everyone and everything that comes within the orbit of its influence, to none more so than to the successful competitor, for the spoils, he finds in the end, do not belong to him; instead, he belongs to the spoils. This is the kind of competition that leads to high frequencies of ulcers and nervous breakdowns; to high delinquency rates, divorce and separation rates, and homicide rates; and to violent crime rates that are the highest in the world — as they are in America.

It has been said that no man is an island because every man is so much at sea. There is a modicum of truth in that statement. No man is an island because every man is involved, by his natural endowment, in every other man. Not only are other men parts of our environment, but they are also *necessary* parts. We are involved not only in other men, but in their welfare — or we should be. The competitive frame of reference is antithetical to such a way of life. It misplaces the emphasis on oneself rather than upon the other, and such value as it affords to one, it validates in terms of externals instead of in terms of internals. The principle of conspicuous consumption — in plain English, keeping up with the Joneses — is perhaps the clearest illustration of the misplaced emphasis. Driving up to your neighbor's house in the "right" car may spell prestige in a society of false values, but the proper value of a man lies, not in the quality of his car, but in the quality of self — the most precious of all his possessions.

In America we have often tended to place too much value on things and not enough on people. This is because we have desired to "arrive" in terms of things rather than in reference to people, a state to which competition inevitably leads.

On the other hand, cooperation, striving *with* others — *not* against them — is a far more efficient way of achieving any objective than competition is. Cooperation seeks to bring out the best in everyone. Competition, in spite of oft-reiterated statements to the contrary, in the long run has the effect of making it impossible for large numbers of individuals to exhibit what is in them. This is where competitive examinations so often fail and where in a cooperatively designed examination much greater justice would be done to the individual, with correspondingly greater benefits accruing to his society.

It is far more efficient to cooperate with one another to help bring out the best that is within us than it is to compete with one another in order to do so. As industry, as well as many another group, is slowly learning, cooperation pays higher dividends than competition does; this is not to say that all competition is bad. Cooperative competition, the kind toward which American industry has been developing, is perhaps better called competitive cooperation, in which different groups, formerly competitors, agree to join forces and cooperate.

AMERICAN VIRTUES: INDIVIDUALISM AND SELF-RELIANCE

George W. Maxey

The following reading was originally delivered as a speech at the commemoration of the three hundredth anniversary of the Swedish settlement on the Delaware, Philadelphia, Pennsylvania, on November 5, 1943. At that time George W. Maxey was Chief Justice of the Pennsylvania Supreme Court.

Think of the following questions while you read:

1. In the author's opinion, what qualities made the early Americans successful in colonizing a strange new land?
2. Why has self-reliance been important in the past? Is it still important in our society?
3. Do you agree with the author's claim that self-denial and self-discipline are necessary?

George W. Maxey, ''The Qualities of the Early Americans,'' **Vital Speeches of the Day**, January 1, 1944, page 170-73. Reprinted with permission.

The Qualities Of Early Americans

All will agree that the people who colonized this new land made a great success of it in spite of many "setbacks." What qualities made them successful? Their chief characteristics, whether they were Cavaliers in Virginia, or Puritans or Pilgrims in Massachusetts, or Swedes along the Delaware, were initiative and industry, self-reliance and courage. They had no paternalistic government to lean on. They were not a protected people; they were a resistant people. They never dedicated themselves to the cult of comfort.

The entire development of this country has depended on the existence of the same qualities which characterized the early settlers. These were the qualities of those who hewed paths through trackless forests and over mountains, who bridged rivers and conquered barren stretches of sand. They were individualists. They faced hostile elements and hostile men with equanimity and fortitude. They had character enough both to respect authority and to resist its abuse.

The signers of the Declaration of Independence and, a little later, of the Constitution, were largely the descendants of hardy pioneers. None of them were born idlers and all of them were contemptuous of a "leisure class." Like all Anglo-Saxons, ever intolerant of governmental strait-jackets, they renounced the rule of George III because it went beyond legitimate bounds in curbing their individual and economic freedom. They asked little of the government except to mind its own business as long as they lawfully minded theirs. They established a Republic where to every man there was opened the rough path to fame and fortune if he had the courage and vigor to tread it, and where above the humblest cradle there ever shone the star of hope. They swept away the aristocracy of idleness and established the nobility of labor. They found their chieftain in a frontier surveyor and pathfinder. His formal education was limited; the halls of higher learning never echoed to his footfalls. But from honest, hardy ancestors who believed that well-doing was the only way to well-being there came to him the best of all inheritances, *character*; and in a youth and early manhood replete with arduous toil and dangerous tasks, he proved himself dependable and steadfast, and developed what Tenny-

son calls ''the wrestling thews that throw the world.''
The stanchest timber is ever found in oaks that have
defied and survived the storms. Neither Washington
nor any of his associates had any illusions about
establishing a government strong enough for everybody to lean on or rich enough for everybody to live on.
They made no pretence of being able to create wealth or
happiness by law. What they fought for and won was
the right of men and women to life, liberty and the
pursuit of happiness. They made no extravagant
promises and raised no vain hopes.

> **The Creator made life a competitive game and
> wherever there is competition there will be those
> who succeed and those who fail.**

Theodore Roosevelt well said: ''No education, no
refinements of civilization can compensate a people for
the loss of their hardy virtues. The greatest danger of a
luxurious civilization,'' said he, ''is that it is likely to
lead a people to lose their fighting edge.'' These hardy
virtues are essential to individual and national
progress. Life always has been and always will be a trial
and a struggle. ''To him who will hear the clarions of
the battle call and on Greatheart forever ring the clang-
ing blows.''

Life Is A Competitive Game

Any man of authority who promises a people that
through legislative magic the struggle of life will be
abolished and that there will be equal rewards for the
indolent and the industrious is not a leader but a
misleader of his people. The Creater made life a competitive game and wherever there is competition there
will be those who succeed and those who fail. To
promise an end to struggle is like promising a man
climbing a mountain an end of the law of gravitation.
Without the law of gravitation we would have celestial
chaos; without the law of struggle we would have
weakness and decadence....

119

It was the scholars of Columbus's day who placed the greatest obstacles in his path as he went from capital to capital arguing that by sailing west he could reach the East. Columbus was an individualist; Washington, Franklin, Jefferson and Lincoln were individualists; so have been all the great inventors; so have been all the other human beings to whom this Nation owes its progress. Individualists are produced in an environment where every day is a day of struggle, where "flags of truce" are seldom sent and even darkness does not always stay the combat....

No parent should so enfeeble its children and no government should so enfeeble its citizens as to unfit them for the battle of life. No individual ever became strong of body and alert of mind by losing his *self*-reliance and relying upon *somebody else*. A feather pillow is a poor substitute for a grindstone in sharpening an axe. No razor ever acquired a cutting edge by being honed on a piece of cheese. Theodore Roosevelt in his address on "The Strenuous Life" said: "I preach not the doctrine of ignoble ease but the doctrine of the strenuous life, the life of toil and effort, of labor and strife. No country can long endure," he said, "if its foundations are not laid deep in the material prosperity which comes from thrift, from business energy and enterprise, from hard, unsparing effort in the fields of industrial activity."...

The greatest asset of any nation is strength of character and it is developed only by work, by self-denial and self-discipline. "Advise me how to rear my son," said a mother to General Robert E. Lee. "Teach him to deny himself," replied the great Virginian. No nation of self-indulgent peoples are under anything like equal conditions a match in war for a nation of self-denying people. The self-denying Macedonians under Alexander, though over-matched in numbers seventeen to one, quickly conquered the self-indulgent Persians. The old Roman was right who said, "An animal whose hoofs are hardened on rough ground can travel any road."

The soundest society is where the individual works out his own salvation, as the pioneers and colonizers of America worked out theirs. No man ever learned to walk by being carried, and a sure way to soften society is to spoon-feed its individuals. Whenever the leaners outnumber the lifters a collapse is imminent. A people whose quest is for rights without responsibilities, jobs without work, freedom without effort, and a country without fighting for it, will not long have any rights, any jobs, any freedom, or any country. Every worth while possession is an achievement — not an endowment. No legislative gadgets are a worthy substitute for old-fashioned virtues. Economic salvation *by statute* and international security *without sacrifice* are twin delusions. The best society is that one which secures to each man a fair opportunity to pursue his own good but does not pursue that good for him. As a director of individual destiny government has always been a failure. The sustenance for American spiritual and material might has been drawn through the roots of individual initiative and enterprise.

CONTEMPORARY AMERICAN HEROES

This exercise will give you an opportunity to see what values you and your classmates consider important by ranking the American heroes listed below. A person's choice of heroes and the reasons for his choice should give him some insight into what is important to him.

© King Features Syndicate 1975

Part I

Instructions

STEP 1. The class should break into groups of four to six students.

STEP 2. Working individually, within each group, each student should rank the Americans listed

123

below, assigning the number (1) to the person whose life style he most admires, the number (2) to the next most admired, and so on, until all Americans have been ranked.

STEP 3. Each student should compare his ranking with others in the group, giving the reasons for his ranking.

STEP 4. The class as a whole should rank the American heroes, using the same procedure as in Step 2.

CONTEMPORARY AMERICAN HEROES

Ralph Nader (crusader for the American Consumer)

Jacqueline Onassis (wife of former President John Kennedy)

John Wayne (movie star)

Billie Jean King (professional tennis player and businesswoman)

Henry Kissinger (U.S. diplomat and Secretary of State)

Hugh Heffner (founder and publisher of **Playboy**)

Mick Jagger (rock musician)

Joe Namath (professional football player)

President of General Motors

Patricia Hearst (alleged critic of American society and former fugitive)

Billy Graham (preacher)

Others

Part II

Instructions

Working either in small groups of four to six students or all together, the class should discuss the Beetle Bailey cartoon.

1. What commentary is it making about television heroes?
2. Do you agree with the cartoon's message?
3. Are T.V. heroes a good example of heroes that most Americans generally admire? What about movie heroes?

THE VALUES OF THE NON-INDIAN WORLD

Ed McGaa

Ed McGaa, an Oglala Sioux, is a lawyer, author, teacher and a former Marine fighter pilot. He is also serving as co-chairman of Minnesota's Bicentennial Commission.

As you read try to answer the following questions:

1. What is the dilemma of the non-Indian world in the author's opinion.
2. Why does Mr. McGaa claim the white man migrated to America?
3. What do the four sacred colors of the American Indian stand for? How do the values they represent differ from the values represented by those who worship gold or green as their sacred colors?
4. What does the author suggest we do in the future? Do you agree?

Ed. McGaa, ''The Dilemma of the Non-Indian World...'' **Dimensions**, Summer, 1973, pp. 14-15. Reprinted with permission from the author.

The dilemma of the non-Indian world is that you have lost respect for your mother — Mother Earth — from whom and where we have all come from.

We all start out in this world as tiny seeds — no different from the trees, the flowers, the winged people, or our animal brothers, the deer, the bear or Tatanka — the buffalo. Every particle of our bodies here today comes from the good things that Mother Earth has put forth.

This morning at breakfast we took from Mother Earth to live as we have done every day of our lives. But did we thank our Mother Earth for giving us the means to live? The old Indian did. When he drove his horse in near to a buffalo running at full speed across the prairie, he drew his bow string back and as he did so, he said, "Forgive me brother but my people must live." After he butchered the buffalo, he would take the skull and face it to the setting sun as a thanksgiving and an acknowledgment that all things come from Mother Earth.

The Indian never took more than he needed. Today the buffalo is gone. It is very late, but there is still time to revive and rediscover the old American Indian value of respect for Mother Earth.

You say Ecology. We think the word Mother Earth has a deeper meaning. If we wish to survive, we must respect her. She is very beautiful and already she is showing us signs that she may punish us for not respecting her. Also, we must remember she has been placed in this universe by the one who is all-powerful, the Great Spirit above or Wakontankan — God.

A few hundred years ago, there lived in this land of Minne-ota — much water — a people, the American Indian, who well knew a respect and value system that enabled him to live here without having to migrate away from his Mother Earth in contrast to the white brother who migrated by the thousands from his Mother Earth because he had developed a different value system from the American Indian.

Carbon dating techniques say we were here for 30,000 to 80,000 years and that if we did migrate, it was because of a natural phenomenon — a glacier — and

not because of a social system that had a few rich controlling many, many poor, causing them to migrate as
happened in Europe from 1500 to the present. We
Indian people say we were always here.

We, the American Indian, had a way of living that
enabled us to live within the great complete beauty that
only the natural environment can provide. The Indian
tribes had a common value system and a commonality
of religion without religious animosity that preserved
that great beauty that man definitely needs. Our four
commandments from the Great Spirit are *Respect for
Mother Earth*, *Respect for the Great Spirit*, *Respect for
Fellow Man* (we are and will continue to be a nonpre-
judiced people) and *Respect for Individual Freedom*,
provided that individual freedom does not threaten the
people, the tribe, or Mother Earth.

Our four sacred colors are red, yellow, black, and
white. They stand for the four directions — red for the
east, yellow for the south, black for the west, and white
for the north. From the east comes the rising sun and
new knowledge from a new day. From the south will
come the warming southwinds that will cause our
mother to bring forth the good foods and grasses so that
we may live. To the west where the sun goes down, the
day will end and we will sleep and we will also hold our
spirit ceremonies at night, from where we will com-
municate with the spirit world beyond. From the north
will come the white winter snow that will cleanse
Mother Earth and put her to sleep so that she may rest
and store up energy to provide the beauty and bounty of
springtime. We will also create through our arts and
crafts during the long winter season.

All good things come from these sacred directions. These sacred directions or four sacred colors also stand for the four races of man — red, white, black, and yellow men. We cannot be a prejudiced people because all men are brothers, because all men have the same mother. You are my white sister and you are my white brother and you are my black brother and my black sister because we have the same mother — Mother Earth. He who is prejudiced and hates another because of his color hates what the Great Spirit has put here. He hates that which is holy and he will be punished even during this lifetime as man will be punished for violating Mother Earth. This is what we Indian people truly believe.

We, the Indian people, also believe that the red man was placed in America by the Great Spirit, the white man in Europe, the black man in Africa, and the yellow man in Asia. What about the brown man? The brown man evolved from the sacred colors coming together. Look at our Mother Earth. She, too, is brown because the four directions have come together. After the Great Spirit, Wakontankan, placed them in their respective areas, he appeared to them in a different manner and taught them ways so that they might live in harmony and true beauty. Some men, some tribes, some nations have still retained the teachings of the Great Spirit. Others have not. (This no doubt shocks some of you Christians who have the stereotype that we Indian people are pagans, savages or heathens, but we do not believe that you control the way to the spirit world that lies beyond.) We believe that the Great Spirit loves all his children equally, although he must be disturbed at times with those of his children who have raped and pillaged Mother Earth because they worshipped gold or

green as their sacred colors and placed materialistic acquisition as their god even to the point of enslaving their fellow man so that they may own and possess more material goods.

Brothers and sisters, we must go back to some of the old ways if we are ever going to truly save our Mother Earth and bring back the natural beauty that every man seriously needs, especially in this day of drugs, tranquilizers, insane asylums, ulcers, extreme poor, extreme rich who share nothing, prisons, jails, rigid boundaries, germ warfare, and complete annihilation weapons.

A great Hunkpapa Sioux chief, Sitting Bull, said to the Indian people, "Take the best of the white man's road, pick it up and take it with you. That which is bad, leave it alone, cast it away. Take the best of the old Indian ways — always keep them. They have been proven for thousands of years. Do not let them die."

My friends, I will never cease being an Indian. I will never cease respecting the old Indian values, especially our four cardinal commandments and the values of generosity and sharing. I believe that the white man became so greedy that he destroyed many things. I also believe that the white man has done a great deal of good in this world. He has good ways and he has bad ways. The good way of the white man's road I am going to keep. The very fact that we can all speak freely, the very fact none of us here are hungry, the very fact that we talk a common language and many of us have come from a great distance and can still exchange knowledge, the fact that we can exchange knowledge immediately over a wire to another country, shows the

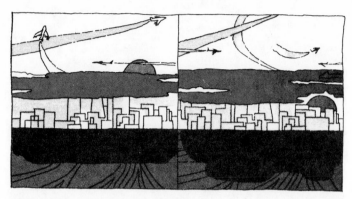

wisdom of my white brothers. These ways I will always keep and cherish, but my white brothers, I say you must give up this materialism to excess. Keep those material goods that you need to exist. Be more of a sharing and a generous person. Have more respect for the aged and family tradition. Have more respect for family that extends not only from mother and father to son and daughter but goes on to grandmothers and grandfathers and aunts and uncles, goes out to the animal world as your brother, to Mother Earth and Father Sky and then to Tankashilah, the Grandfather.

Tankashilah means Grandfather. Wakontankan means the Great Spirit. They are both the same. When we pray directly to God, we say Tankashilah because we are so family-minded that we think of Him as our Grandfather and we are His grandchildren. And, of course, Mother Earth is our mother because Grandfather intended it so. This is a part of the great deep feeling and psychology that we have as Indian people. It is why we preserved and respected our environment for such a long period.

Remember that Mother Earth is truly a holy being and that all things in this world are holy and must not be violated and that we must share and be generous with one another. You may call it in your fancy words psychology, theology, sociology, or philosophy. Call it whatever you wish, but think of Mother Earth as a living being. Think of your fellow man as a holy person who was put here by the Great Spirit being, of the four sacred colors. And think of brown also as a sacred color. You will be far more successful as a nation.

Only with the thought that Mother Earth is truly a

holy being, and that all things in this world are holy and must not be violated and that we must share and be generous with one another — only with this thought — you must think of Mother Earth as a living being. Think of your fellow man as a holy person who was put here by the Great Spirit Being and think of the four sacred colors. With this philosophy in mind you will be far more successful to truly understand the Indian's respect for Mother Earth.

SPORTS MIRROR AMERICAN VALUES

Robert J. Bueter

Fr. Bueter is a Jesuit priest and chairman of the theology department of Loyola Academy in Wilmette, Illinois. He was ordained in June of 1973 and was the editor of **The National Jesuit News**, an inter-province Jesuit paper, from 1972 until 1975.

The following questions should help you examine the reading:

1. Why does the author believe that sports mirror American values?
2. What kind of values did Vince Lombardi, the former coach of the Green Bay Packers, exemplify?
3. What is the goal of middle-class values, and how does it relate to football and the Lombardi approach?
4. What two conclusions does the author come to about current attitudes concerning American values?

Robert J. Bueter, ''Sports, Values and Society,'' **Christian Century**, April 5, 1972, pp. 389-91. Copyright 1972 Christian Century Foundation. Reprinted by permission from the April 5, 1972 issue of **The Christian Century**.

The various values that Americans live by have been defended and debunked with much energy and earnestness in recent years. The value debate has even invaded the realm of sports, which indeed are a big part of Americans' lives — they preoccupy our children, pre-empt our television screen and pour huge sums of money into our economy. The current literature about sports, therefore, may tell us something about the ideals of man and the visions of society that motivate both those who praise and those who condemn or poke fun at the American sports world, and at the same time may help us to understand our own values. Appropriately — for that is where more and more Americans are spending their time and money — it is on football that most of this literature centers.

The World of Vince Lombardi

In 1970 Jerry Kramer, the All-Pro Green Bay guard whose **Instant Replay** and **Farewell to Football** took us behind the professional football scene, edited a book titled **Lombardi: Winning Is the Only Thing**, a memorial to the late great coach who was the dominant figure in professional football and in American sports generally during the '60s. In this book 23 men who knew Vince Lombardi well talk about him and what he represented. One of them — Frank Gifford, star of the New York football Giants and well known television sportscaster for ABC — laments American youth's indifference to the values Lombardi stood for. "Kids today don't fight like we did," he writes (p. 62). "They can play football and basketball like hell, but they're very gentle... They're out playing for fun, and it's not going to interfere with their demonstration for the week or with the things they consider important. If you... dropped them under Lombardi, they might say 'What the hell is he talking about?' They wouldn't understand." Another contributor to the book — Bart Starr, the quarterback of Lombardi's greatest teams — agrees that young people are losing the values that made Vince and America great: mental toughness, commitment to excellence, determination to win, pride, loyalty, self-sacrifice, dedication and religion.

That youth becomes the focus of sportsmen's discussion of values seems fitting. Not only is competitive athletics a field primarily reserved for the young, but the shift in America's values is best exemplified in our young people's life style. The values that Gifford, Starr and other contributors to the Lombardi book single out as important are the very values that, they fear, today's youth are repudiating.

This whole set of values is what many describe as "middle class." Let us try to analyze them according to their goal and the means and manner of attaining it.

The goal of middle-class values is success; that is, increasing accumulation of goods leading to higher social status. The means of success is hard work and continual striving on the part of the individual — a means that necessarily fosters elitism and class consciousness. The manner is basically puritanical: disciplined repression of present needs for the sake of future gratification, commitment to law and order accompanied by reliance on authority and tradition, and an optimistic pragmatism whose methods are always open to change.

Now, these are exactly the values that, as his admirers see it, were fundamental in the world of Vince Lombardi. He was a good coach because he was successful; he accumulated a lot of goods for the players who were fortunate enough to be part of his Packer family. He relied on individual hard work and discipline, and instilled in his men the consciousness that they were better and must achieve according to their elite status. His manner was hard and puritanical: he drove his men to their limits, promising them "success" in return. He was strictly authoritarian, yet he was an optimistic pragmatist in his ability to adjust to individuals and situations. But are the values Lombardi represented the ones that young people live by today? Gifford and Starr think not.

Dave Meggyesy doesn't think so either. But in his opinion this is a good thing. Meggyesy, a former All-Pro linebacker with the St. Louis football Cardinals, says in his book **Out of Their League** that young people are right in rejecting the value system of American society. Indeed, he calls for a revolution in values, for a radical transformation of our society that would make it free, just and humane. And in that society, he says, football would be obsolete — at least football as it now operates. Out of his own experience, Meggyesy cites

135

some of the shameful facts about college and professional football; e.g., the drug usage and the racist policies and practices.

FOOTBALL IS DEHUMANIZING

After playing the sport most of my life, I've come to see that football is one of the most dehumanizing experiences a person can face, and in this book I'm going to tell you what's really behind the video glitter of the game — the racism and fraud, the unbelievable brutality that affects mind as much as body. To me, it is no accident that Richard Nixon, the most repressive President in American history, is a football freak, and that the sport is rapidly becoming our version of bread and circuses.

Dave Meggyesy, **Out of Their League** (Berkeley, California: Ramparts Press, Inc., 1970), p. 6.

Coerced into Conformity

Jack Scott, whose Center for the Study of Sport and Society sponsored Meggyesy's book, repeats these charges in his own book **The Athletic Revolution**. Of the abuses that he says are rampant in college athletics, he mentions particularly the crass and pressurized recruiting, which involves everything from easy sex to junketeering; the lack of concern on the part of coaches for their players' education (many athletes get little time for study; some are given stolen tests or have others take exams for them); the coaches' intrusion into the private lives of the athletes by laying down petty rules governing personal appearance and life style. Summing up, Scott accuses the college "athletic establishment" — administrators, coaches and alumni — of using the athletes to further their own personal and corporate goals.

But these abuses are not Scott's main point. Like Meggyesy, he sees athletics as a symbol of a society whose values are bankrupt. However, Scott asserts that athletics is not only a symbol and a reinforcement of a basically unsound value system, but also one of the principal ways by which young people are socialized into that system. The college athlete, he charges, is not encouraged to develop democratically as a free individual and to set up his own values and goals regardless of society's; instead, he is coerced into conformity with the values, goals and expectations of the people who control the highly authoritarian, militaristic and totalitarian environment. Scott goes so far as to compare American with Russian athletics: Give me a boy, he says, and in Russia I'll give you back a good communist and in America a good capitalist.

A Revolution in Awareness?

Here we are at the heart of the current critique of American middle-class values. It is a widespread critique, deep and serious. Charles Reich, for example, asserts that those values have created a monster, the "corporate state." But he claims that a revolution in human awareness is coming — a revolution that will produce a new man and a new society, endowed with imagination and vitality and a strong sense of selfhood. In short, Reich and a host of others are saying that American society is at a crossroads, on the verge of a revolution in values. For their part, such critics of athletics as Scott and Meggyesy are pointing out that football and organized sports in general are one of the bastions of the evil old order and must be stormed before the revolution can take place.

The values the revolutionists defend can be analyzed under the three headings we applied to middle-class values: their goal, their means and their manner. The goal of the new values is not success — accumulation of goods and all that this entails — but rather the development and cultivation of the person, his growth in awareness and inner peace. The means is not individual striving but rather group participation and cooperation, communal sharing, and mutual engagement with experimental culture forms — all of which lead not to class-consciousness but to increasing openness and acceptance of others. The manner is not puritanical but sensual: gratification is immediate, suppression and discipline give way to free expression, and optimistic pragmatism is replaced by a utopianism that, to be

WHAT'S WRONG
WITH BEING SECOND?

Over a period of 13 years, a certain major-league baseball team had the best over-all won-lost record in its league, including five straight second-place finishes. During that period, the team came to be characterized as "losers."

For five straight years a certain professional football team won its division championship and then was eliminated either in the play-offs or, finally, in the Super Bowl itself.

And what was said of that fine football team during this period of unprecedented winning? They "couldn't win the big ones." They were, you see, just losers.

In this Alice in Wonderland world we have fallen into, there is only one thing that really counts — that is, winning the Super Bowl, being No. 1. All else is empty, meaningless.

And even after you've just won the Super Bowl — *especially* after you've just won the Super Bowl — *there's always next year.* So you see, this way of thinking makes us — all of us — into eventual losers.

We only have to look back into history to see where the mindless worship of hot competition can lead. The ancient Olympics, under the encroachment of professionalism, with its demand for winning at all costs, gradually fell prey to bribery and other forms of corruption. By the time of Alexander the Great, Olympic athletes were held in disrepute.

Under Roman domination, the games themselves were disgraced. The Emperor Nero, for example, fell out of his chariot twice during one

> Olympic race and finally had to give up. In an act of irony appropriate to the downfall of ancient ideals, the judges then awarded him the olive crown of victory.
>
> We have by no means sunk so low — but we might well face up to the worst aspects of our own situation where the sports boom is concerned: Our current overemphasis on competitive team sports is making us a nation of weaklings. Our current overemphasis on "winning" is making us a nation of losers.

Taken from George B. Leonard, "False Worship of Winning," **Minneapolis Tribune**, April 11, 1975.

sure, is somewhat pessimistic and nihilistic. Thus the new values repudiate authority and tradition in favor of protest and social change, and they reject technology with its props of elitism and class consciousness.

Obviously, these values are a threat to football and other sports as we know them. (We can't imagine Vince Lombardi saying,"Inner awareness isn't everything, it's the *only* thing.") But they are the values that have driven men like Meggyesy and others out of football and into the radical counterculture. Jack Scott is one of those who think that the new culture will reform sports as well as all other fields of endeavor. In "Running as a Spiritual Experience," a short essay he appends to his **The Athletic Revolution**, Scott says that sports, besides being a gratifying and immediately enjoyable experience, can foster the group spirit and at the same time develop the individual participant's awareness of himself....

Saturday Swinger, Sunday Charger

Another young man who plays football — Marty Domres, a quarterback for the San Diego Chargers — takes a far easier view of pro football and American society. His book **Bump and Run** is billed as the story of a "Saturday Swinger and Sunday Charger." The title refers not to the on-the-field maneuver of *bump*ing a pass receiver at the line of scrimmage before *run*ning downfield with him, but to the off-the-field caper of throwing a pass at a girl, scoring in her bed, and getting back to your own in time for curfew check. Slick and saucy stuff, this. But incidentally Domres does talk about the question before us. The authoritarian structure of football and other sports doesn't bother him; it takes a "slave-driver" to keep the athlete in form, he says. In other words, he will use the means necessary to win the goal and will endure the manner. His acceptance of these middle-class values, however, does not blind Domres to the evils of American society. He expresses concern over hunger, poverty, loneliness, war, racism, drugs, and says he wants to do something about them after his lucky days of playing for pay are over. But with that he stops.

Here is the striking contrast between Domres and Meggyesy. Both have been through the same system and have seen the same evils, but have come up with different responses to it. Meggyesy has rejected the system and turned radical. Domres has found personal satisfaction in the system: he is proud of his college and his education, he is grateful to his coaches, and he *likes* playing the violent game that, after all, has rewarded him well.

The contrast between these two young men points up two important facts about current attitudes concerning American values. First, most critics tend to put all young people on one side of the debate and all older people on the other. But the evidence is that the division is not that clear-cut. Not all young people are part of the so-called counterculture, and the many differences among them revolve precisely around values. Second, if Meggyesy and Domres can in the main agree about the evils of American society and of the football system, their basic disagreement must be attributed to their differing value system. Both see the same situation, but each interprets it in the light of his own views of what is desirable. Hence we conclude, first, that there is no monolithic youth response to America's moral problem; and second, that the nature of values is such that they must be freely chosen and lived by. Values cannot be legislated or forced upon us. Therefore the important thing is that we make a clear choice and stick by it.

OUR DOMINANT CULTURAL VALUES

Cora DuBois

Cora DuBois is an anthropologist and educator. She has graduate degrees from Columbia, the University of California and other schools. She has taught at Columbia, Sara Lawrence, Harvard and Radcliffe, and served as Professor Emeritus at Cornell. She is the winner of several awards for scholarship and has authored numerous books and journal monographs.

Consider the following questions while reading:

1. How is work a specific value in American society, in Dr. Dubois' opinion?
2. How does materialism figure into our value system?
3. Dr. DuBois claims conformity has replaced liberty as a focal value in our society. What does she mean?

Cora DuBois, ''The Dominant Value Profile of American Culture,'' **American Anthropologist**, December 1955, pp. 1232-39. Reproduced by permission of the American Anthropological Association from the **American Anthropologist** 57 (6), 1955.

1. Effort-Optimism

Work is a specific value in American society. It is not so much a necessary condition of existence as a positive good.... Work becomes a goal in itself and in the process may acquire the quality of activity for its own sake. Thus recreation, although theoretically the antithesis of work, nevertheless in its activism shows many of the aspects of work. "Fun" is something that most Americans work hard for and at, so that they must be warned at forty to give up tennis for golf, or hunting trips for painting. Touring, whether at home or abroad, acquires the quality of a marathon. And this in turn is closely associated with another specific value linked with the effort-optimism syndrome, the importance placed on education. However, as we shall see later, the education effort acquires a particularly American case when taken in conjunction with the other two focal values, material well-being and conformity. In sum, as many foreigners have observed, American life gives the impression of activism. The directives, as well as the virtues and vices, associated with this optimistic activism are numerous: "If at first you don't succeed, try, try again"; or, in the more contemporary idiom, "Let's get this show on the road." The optimistic quality that pervades the American mood is clearly conveyed by the "bigger ergo better" mentality; the "never say die"; the "up and at 'em."

Vigor, at least as motility, connotes biologic youth. The cult of youthfulness in this society is again a specific value frequently commented upon by foreign observers. This observation is borne out by the popularity of the heroes manufactured in Hollywood and in the world of sports, by the advertisements of styles and cosmetics. As the average age of the population increases, this value is already showing signs of being given new interpretations in terms of geriatrics, etc....

2. Material Well-Being

If indeed effort is optimistically viewed in a material universe that man can master, then material well-being is a consistent concomitant value. Not only is it consistent within the value system, but it has been amply demonstrated in our national experience. It has been manifest in the American standard of living. The

Drawing by W. Miller; © 1973 The New Yorker Magazine, Inc.

nation's geographic frontier and its natural resources, combined with an era of invention, have convinced most Americans of the validity of such a proposition. In the American scene progress and prosperity have come to have almost identical meaning. So deeply convinced are most Americans of what is generally called "prosperity" that material well-being is close to being considered a "right" due to those who have conscientiously practiced the specific value of work. The congruence of this view with the new science of geriatrics, social insurance, and the growth of investment trusts is obvious....

One of the most common stereotypes about the United States is its materialism. Viewed in the context of the value system presented here, materialism is less a value *per se* than an optimistic assertion of two value premises (mastery over material nature and the perfectibility of man) that have operated in a favorable environment. What foreign observers may call materialism, with derogatory or envious innuendos, is to the American a success that carries the moral connotation of "rightness" — of a system that proves itself or, as Americans would say with complete consistency, that "works." Within the frame of American value premises, success phrased as material well-being re-solves the material-spiritual opposition and becomes a proof of right-mindedness. "Hard work pays off." The old and widely known proverb that "Virtue is its own reward" has a particularly American slant, meaning not that virtue is in itself a reward but rather that virtue is rewarded.

If hard work is a "good thing" in a material universe and since it has been rewarded by material well-being, consistency requires that manual labor should be accorded dignity or, at least, should not be considered undignified. Furthermore, manual labor is an unam-biguous manifestation of that activism alluded to earlier.

The salience of material well-being as a focal value in American life leads into many by-ways, some of which confuse and confound members of societies founded on a different value configuration. In military terms, for example, Americans are so profoundly con-vinced of the correctness of the material well-being formula that logistics forms our basic strategy. Personal heroism, though it may amply exist, is not assumed to be the fundamental requisite for victory, as it is in France. In American terms, victory is won by the sheet of material laid down in front of advancing in-fantry and by the lines of supply that must be built up to provide such a barrier between hand-to-hand combat.

In the same vein, there is little room in the American middle-class value system for the realities of physical pain, brutality, and death. Since they are nonetheless natural and undeniable, they are given a highly stylized treatment in detective fiction, newspapers, and movies that provide an acceptable discharge of tension created by the discrepancy between values and reality. Many Americans are alienated and morally repelled when they encounter the poverty and misery prevalent in certain lands. They manage to go through life un-touched experientially even by those in our own popula-tion who have not succeeded — those who exist hope-lessly in rural or urban slums or those who are victims of physical or psychic disasters. We have provided for the latter so effectively that they are whisked away into institutions that our national surpluses permit us to provide comparatively lavishly. Death itself has been surrounded with appurtenances of asepsis. Evelyn

Waugh's **The Loved One** could never have been written with India as a setting....

3. Conformity

Viewed historically it seems probable that conformity is a more recent focal value in American culture than effort-optimism and material well-being.... Over a century ago De Tocqueville saw with singular clarity the potential threat to national solidarity inherent in the values of individual liberty, on the one hand, and of the sovereignty of enfranchised masses, on the other hand. In the contemporary American value system, conformity represents an attempt to resolve this dilemma. The France of today, with a comparable dilemma, has still to find a resolution.

If the premises of perfectibility and equality are linked with the focal value labeled effort-optimism, then each middle-class American may legitimately aspire to maximal self-realization. But, if man is to master through his efforts a mechanistic universe, he must cooperate with his fellowmen, since no single man can master the universal machine. In other words, people are individuated and prized, but if they are to cooperate with their fellowmen for mastery of the universe or, in more modest terms, of the immediate physical and sociopolitical environment, too great a degree of individualization would be an impediment. Also since the American value premises — in contradistinction to much of the rest of the world — include equality, the realization of the self in such a context would not necessarily imply the development of highly personalized and idiosyncratic but rather of egalitarian traits. Self-cultivation in America has as its goal less the achievement of uniqueness and more the achievement of similarity....

Earlier in our history self-reliance and initiative were specific values attached to the focal value of liberty. Today these specific values have a new focus. Individual self-reliance and initiative are attached to the promotion of the commonweal and to the progress of society. Conformity has replaced liberty as a focal value to which these specific traits are attached. Cooperation has been added as a specific value that has facilitated the shift-over. The present American value

"THEY'LL NEVER GET ME INTO UNIFORM!"

system manifests a highly effective integration of the individual to society....

Education is envisaged as a means by which all men through effort can realize themselves. But since co-operativeness is a specific value also asserted into this equation, education comes to be envisaged as a means to make more men more effective workers and better citizens. The land-grant colleges, the vast network of public schools, and the system of free and compulsory

146

education with its stress on education for citizenship and on technical skills have set the American educational system apart from that of many other countries. In the American context the linkage between conformity, effort-optimism, and material well-being leads inevitably to mass education with the emphasis on the common man rather than the uncommon man, to its technical and practical cast, to what seems to many observers its low standards. Simultaneously, to many Americans schooling has acquired the weight of a goal rather than a means. A college degree is a "good thing" in itself, whether or not the education entailed is prized. This concatenation does not lead one to expect perfection as a directive for performance in American life.

In a society where cooperation and good citizenship are valued and where the commonweal is served by having each man develop himself through his own efforts, a generous friendliness, openness, and relaxation of interpersonal relations are not only possible but desirable so long as the associated expanding economy furnishes the situational possibilities. Rigid class structures and protective privacies are inconsistent with the values here enumerated. Doors need not be closed to rooms; fences need not be built around properties. The tall hedges of England and the enclosing walls of France are not appropriate to the American scene, where life faces outward rather than inward. If every individual is as "good as" the next and all are good citizens — what is there to hide? The open front yards, the porches, or more recently the picture windows that leave the home open to everyone's view, the figurative and literal klieg lights under which our public figures live are all evidence of the value placed in American life on likeness and the pressure exerted for conformity. This is very different from saying that American middle-class individuals are in fact all alike. It means merely that likeness is valued.

EXERCISE **6**

RECOGNIZING ETHNOCENTRIC STATEMENTS

Ethnocentrism is the tendency for people to feel their race, religion, culture, or nation is superior, and to judge others by one's own frame of reference. **Frame of reference** means the standards and values a person accepts because of his life experience and culture. A Marxist in Russia, for example, is likely to view things differently than a democrat in America.

Ethnocentrism has promoted much misunderstanding and conflict. It helps emphasize cultural differences and the notion that your nation's institutions are superior. Education, however, should stress the similarities of the human condition throughout the world and the basic equality and dignity of all men.

In order to avoid war and violence, people must realize how **ethnocentrism** and **frame of reference** limit their ability to be objective and understanding. Consider each of the following statements carefully. Mark **E** for any statements you think is ethnocentric. Mark **N** for any statement you think is not ethnocentric. Mark **U** if you are undecided about any statement.

E = Ethnocentric
N = Not Ethnocentric
U = Undecided

_____ 1. Business is today the most significant force shaping American life.

_____ 2. We Indians have a more human philosophy of life. We Indians will show this country how to act human.

_____ 3. I maintain that certain general but essential orientations of the Gospel Way and the American Way are contradictory.

_____ 4. Our country, by almost any measure, is preeminent in the world.

_____ 5. This competitive system of ours has achieved results beyond man's imagining.

_____ 6. Americans, as a direct result of the individual freedom specified by the Constitution and the Bill of Rights, have earned the greatest degree of security ever enjoyed by any people anywhere.

_____ 7. The American character has softened, weakened, grown feeble with age.

_____ 8. America is the land of the free.

_____ 9. The United States has the best economic system in the world.

_____ 10. America is the "new Israel;" a people chosen by God.

_____ 11. The United States has the most powerful military force in the world.

_____ 12. Our high productivity gives us a high standard of living that is proverbial.

_____ 13. American democracy is a more workable system than communism as practiced in Russia.

5CHAPTER

AMERICAN RELIGIOUS VALUES

Readings
18. **Religion and America's Moral Crisis**
    Eugene B. Borowitz
19. **Whatever Became of Sin?**
    Karl Menninger
20. **Sports and Religion**
    Cornish Rogers
21. **America's Civil Religion**
    Robert Bellah

RELIGION AND AMERICA'S MORAL CRISIS

Eugene B. Borowitz

Eugene B. Borowitz is a member of **Worldview's** editorial board. **Worldview** is a journal published by the Council on Religion and International Affairs. Dr. Borowitz is also professor of Education and Jewish Religious Thought at Hebrew Union College. He is an author who most recently published **The Mask Jews Wear**.

Consider the following questions while reading:

1. What does Mr. Borowitz see as America's religious and moral crisis?
2. What does the author claim most Americans have believed in, in the past?
3. What does the author mean when he says that "many people today are amoral?"
4. Why does the author believe America is experiencing a resurgence of spirituality? How does he feel Judaism and Christianity can help America?
5. Do you agree with the author's appraisal of America's religious situation?

Eugene B. Borowitz, "Religion and America's Moral Crisis," **Worldview**, November 1974, pp. 52-56. Reprinted with permission.

A Misplaced Faith

There is a crisis in public morality....

I see our problem less as one of ethics than of metaethics. Our difficulty is not rules or values. There are so many of them around that our difficulty is in choosing among them. Worse, it is in caring at all about being moral. I suggest that our ethics have become so anemic because they have lost their support system. More, I shall argue that our characterological breakdown is the result of misplaced faith.

Let me begin my analysis of our condition by applying to it Paul Tillich's understanding of what it means to be religious. For him, and for me in this stage of the investigation, one's religion is best thought of in existentialist terms: What is, in fact, one's ultimate concern? This is an untraditional and uninstitutional way of thinking about having faith. For all its novelty, it is highly appropriate to our task, for we are concerned with the moral crisis of our civilization and thus require a tool which enables us to understand how believers and unbelievers alike have caught the plague....

What has been the operative faith of most Americans for the past generation or so? Note that the question is not, What would people say to a pollster?, nor even In what religious buildings might they, with some frequency, be found? When we inquire about ultimate concern we reach far beneath the level of conventional behavior or locations. We ask, rather: When people were faced by significant, demanding choices, to what did they give the major free energies of their lives? What did they really care about more than anything else?...

What most Americans have believed in, I submit, was not God or Church or Torah but the burgeoning American society. In simple terms, we put our trust in ever greater affluence: once deprived, we gained sufficiency, once degraded by unceasing want, we came to the self-respect of a steady, decent income. For us Exodus or Resurrection was the liberation from a slum flat to clean rooms, thence to a decent neighborhood, a garden apartment perhaps, or on to a home in the suburbs, even a second home. This process, repeated on many levels, promised not only satisfaction but, in its own way, salvation.

I do not mean to describe us as merely economic animals. We were, amidst our upward social striving, also concerned about the quality of our existence. In our aspirations for our families we can most easily see the close relationship between greater good and greater goods. And a similar broad sense of the promise of growth was felt in other areas of our civilization. We looked to schooling not only as preparation for a good job but also for a richer life. So as adults we turn to books and records and magazines and concerts and hobbies to deepen our minds and increase our sensitivity. The arts would give us character; recreation would restore our soul. Psychiatry would solve our personal problems, science our technical ones, politics and community work our social ones.

By calling this a misplaced faith I do not mean to denigrate these activities. They were, and are, legitimate concerns, productive of much that is morally worthwhile. The question is: Is this complex of interests and values worthy of our ultimate trust? Does it create and sustain the morals it contains, or must they be drawn from another, deeper source? Can the American way of life bear the full weight of our ethical existence, or must it derive its sense of quality and direction from something that lies beyond it, a "more ultimate" concern?

> **Our science is value-free, our economics interested in profit, our politics concerned with power, our arts dominated by questions of technique, our lifestyle devoted to strategies of escape and indulgence.**

The Idol of Secularity

The key issue here is the power of secularity. We had put our trust in man and his capacities. That is, our ultimate hope was in ourselves, singly and jointly. Either we abandoned the God of the Bible or made God

153

marginal to more significant concerns. In either case we based our lives and our values on our secularity, and it is this, our old, fundamental, existential faith, that has now been thrown into question. For it is no longer clear that secularity mandates morality. To the contrary, it seems abundantly clear that secularity is compatible with amorality and can even accommodate and encourage immorality, by the standards of the Bible....

For most of us the new realism about secularity began with a changing sense of perspective. Instead of taking certain rules or institutions for granted as exemplars of ethical practice, we began asking what, in truth, they did to people. Segregation was the classic case. It had claimed the sanction of law, tradition, established practice, and the apparent will of the majority of voters in a wide region. But when we got down to thinking about what it was doing to people, we knew it to be wrong. We knew that when one cannot think of a certain group of people as persons, entitled to the rights of all persons, then one is immoral. And that from the perspective of being a person, the great good is freedom, the great goal is being true to oneself. We also came to see the great problem in human relations as power and its abuse: If you use your power over me to constrain my freedom you render me less a person....

With persons as the criterion of the good, with power seen as a common force for the bad, a new moral realism began to dawn on us. The institutions whose goodness we had taken for granted now showed themselves to be run by relatively insensitive power, and thus to be injurious to persons. We became aware of tyrannies we had never before noted, at home, at school, in business, in sports, in our social relationships and our politics....

More disturbing, it began to dawn on us that the morality we thought was demanded by our secular culture was only another option to it. What was there in a secular view of things that could mandate concern for all other persons as well as self-interest? Why should we indeed care for the weak and the powerless, the ungainly and unattractive, the failures and the bores, as long as we get what we want? Our science is value-free, our economics interested in profit, our politics concerned with power, our arts dominated by questions of technique, our lifestyle devoted to strategies of escape and indulgence.

Perhaps we might have come to terms with that, for people have often lived poorly in the name of great ideals. But secularity also took away our sense of guilt. Ethics became reduced to conditioning, to convention, to education, to psychic mechanism — anything but a commandment, a duty, a summons.

A great part of our crisis, then, is that many people today are effectively amoral. In Freud's day neurosis was most commonly traceable to an oppressive sense of duty and guilt. Today it is more commonly associated with having no firm set of values and by having no sense of limits or direction, thus having no true sense of self at all.

Another part of our crisis is that those of us who still retain a strong sense of biblical morality suddenly feel alien and ill at ease. The moral America we took for granted is not the America we see around us. We are depressed and sickened by its strange hospitality to evil acts and evil people. Our civilization has become our problem — how then can it continue to deserve our existential faith? We now stand in judgment over the secularity which once comprised our ultimate concern. How can we any longer put our most basic trust in it? We are deeply disturbed because we have lost our faith. We believed in a god who was no god. The idol of secularity has fallen, and we are shaken to our core....

Many of the concerns of secularity are legitimate and remain morally compelling. My major quarrel with it derives from its being made a god.

No, America is not all bad, but at the very least it has lost heart. It still does many good things, but it isn't sure they still count. It no longer knows what to care about. It isn't even certain that caring itself still makes much sense.

Yet, paradoxically enough, this moment of doubt creates a new openness to a more adequate religious faith. Insofar as we are deeply disturbed we evidence deep moral concern. We show that somehow we know our ethical values are right, for it is in the name of those values that we deny the old idolatry. We have here the dawning recognition that our ethical commitments transcend us and our society, though we had, for a while, lost sight of that. We are now willing to search for a faith adequate to this new sense of personal depth.

155

Apparently a good many people in our country share this feeling, for we live in a time of unprecedented American religious search....

A Resurgence of Spirituality

America is experiencing a resurgence of spirituality. One might almost call it a rebirth of enthusiasm, in the technical sense of that term, were it not that much of this movement is highly personal, determinedly quiet, and deeply suspicious of religious institutions. Indeed, many people touched by it are afraid to share their quest with others, despite their longing for community, lest public exposure kill the tender shoots of their spirituality. The dramatic manifestations of this surge

NO SOCIETY CAN SURVIVE WITHOUT A RELIGION

No man can live and no society can survive for very long without a religion and a faith of some sort that explains man's nature and the meaning of his life and death. I agree entirely with Toynbee that the history of civilization is the history of society's religions. By "religion" I mean any system of thought and belief that "ties things together" and gives a society something which explains to its satisfaction the meaning of life and death, of good and evil, and of man's own nature.

Communism was such a religion to many young people in my youth. So, in Germany, was Nazism. It's hard to make a religion of democracy, because it's such a flexible system. Besides, democracy as we know it in the West is the political formulation of our Judeo-Christian ideas about the nature of man. We are bound to lose democracy in proportion as we desert our Judeo-Christian religious beliefs and values. And I'm afraid that may be what is happening now.

Clare Boothe Luce, former congresswoman and Ambassador to Italy.

are regularly brought to us by the media: the more established Asian cults like Vedanta and Zen, as well as the currently fashionable sects like those of the Maharishi or the Maharaj Ji. And in our own communities we see extraordinary signs: Catholics who are charismatics; Protestants who as Jesus people turn legalistic, while others from sophisticated churches talk in tongues and heal by faith; and Jews who take a fresh interest in Hasidic devotion and Orthodox discipline.

I submit that these phenomena arise from a sense of the new emptiness at the heart of our culture. They are a desperate, sometimes unthinking, effort to fill it. And something similar may be seen as far away as the Soviet Union.

What Judaism and Christianity can uniquely bring to the American culture at this juncture (in other areas of the world we should, of course, have to add Islam) is their root religious intuition that a transcendent God stands over against us and our society, summoning us to moral conduct. These biblical religions proclaim, against almost all of Asian religious teaching, that God's ultimate character, insofar as humans may speak of such exalted matters, is not neutral. The Lord we serve is not finally beyond the categories of good and evil. Our God is not to be approached through a realm that ultimately lies beyond morality. God's holiness is intimately linked with God's ethical command. There is a direct movement from ''You shall be holy for I the Lord, your God, am holy'' to ''You shall not hate your brother in your heart but you shall love your neighbor as yourself.''...

We Jews and Christians will argue between us and among ourselves whether the new or old law is in effect and in what mode it is to be followed. We shall differ as to the form and nature of the commandments. But I think we will both insist that those who know God should devote themselves to doing good and those who love God ought to love people and dedicate their lives to creating a humane and holy social order....

In secularizing our culture in the past generation or so we have carried out an experiment, so to speak, to see what might happen to our way of life if we abandoned the Judeo-Christian view of human obligation. We did not do too badly for a while. Our commitments to our biblical past run so deep that despite our putative secularity we remain quite faithful to biblical values; much of the remaining moral content of our culture is there, I would argue, not because it is intrinsic to secularity, but as an inheritance from an earlier, more religious age. Only now is it clear what cutting ourselves off from our transcendent source of values does to us and our society.

I am not saying that if all Americans were instantly to take up Jewish and Christian religous duties or, better, were to share Jewish or Christian faith and the ethical responsibilities they entail, all the moral problems of America would be solved. The question of the ground of our values is only one of the many difficulties facing this nation. But it is our root problem. I do not see how, until we reestablish our ultimate sense of why we ought to do the good and in what direction that good lies, the rest of our moral efforts can hope to succeed....

I do not see that we can approach this challenge with any special confidence. We have been tried in the past and found wanting. We must acknowledge that it is quite possible that this beloved country of ours, and we with it, have passed by the moment of our highest moral potential and entered into a period of moral stagnation, if not decline. The crisis is real, our loss may be quite serious indeed. But for all their realism, Judaism and Christianity are religions of hope. We not only believe in the coming of God's kingdom, we believe that, with God's help, we can live in it here and now. It is our difficult task in this difficult hour to live in the reality of God's rule despite all pessimism, and by our words and deeds to summon people from their sinfulness to God's steady service.

WHATEVER BECAME OF SIN?

Karl Menninger

Karl Menninger is a noted psychiatrist and author. He is Senior Consultant to the Stone-Brandel Center in Chicago and Chairman of the Board of Trustees of The Menninger Foundation in Topeka. Some of his books are **A Psychiatrist's World**, **Love Against Hate**, **The Vital Balance**, **The Crime of Punishment**, and most recently, **Whatever Became of Sin?**

The following questions should help you examine the reading:

1. What does Dr. Menninger mean when he claims sin has disappeared in our society?
2. What does he refer to when he uses the term sin?
3. What does he propose?

Karl Menninger, **Whatever Became of Sin** (New York: Hawthorn Books, Inc., 1973), pp. 8-17, 46, 178. Reprinted by permission of Hawthorn Books, Inc. from **Whatever Became of Sin?** by Karl Menninger, M.D. Copyright © 1973 by Karl Menninger, M.D. All rights reserved.

What Ails The American Spirit?

"What ails the American spirit?" an editor asked of some of our seers. "It is the age of rubbish," answered one. "Religion just doesn't play the role it used to play.... Few other things...can hold the culture together.... Young people don't have anything that they want to do....they haven't decided what they want their lives to say."

"The malaise of the American spirit," declared a professor of government, "cannot be blamed on wrong-headed policies, inept administrations, or even an inability to understand the dimensions of our current discontents. The reasons are more fundamental...arising from the kind of people we have become....we cannot bring ourselves to make the personal sacrifices required to sustain domestic order or international authority."...

Daniel J. Boorstin, director of the National Museum of Science and Technology at the Smithsonian Institution, puts our current situation this way: "...we have lost our sense of history....lost our traditional respect for the wisdom of ancestors and the culture of kindred nations.... Flooded by screaming headlines and hourly televised 'news' melodramas of dissent and 'revolution,' we haunt ourselves with the illusory ideal of some 'whole nation' which had a deep and outspoken 'faith' in its 'values.' "...

Well, that's what some of our prophets are saying today. The reporters wrote it down for all to read. Many others have spoken and written similarly....

The Disappearance Of Sin

In all of the laments and reproaches made by our seers and prophets, one misses any mention of "sin," a word which used to be a veritable watchword of prophets. It was a word once in everyone's mind, but now rarely if ever heard. Does that mean that no sin is involved in all our troubles — sin with an "I" in the middle? Is no one any longer guilty of anything? Guilty perhaps of a sin that could be repented and repaired or atoned for? Is it only that someone may be stupid or sick or criminal — or asleep? Wrong things are being

THE SIN OF AFFLUENCE

"It is preoccupation with possession," said Bertrand Russell "more than anything else that prevents men from living freely and nobly."

This was a profound conclusion by a very wise man; does it receive any serious consideration?...

Greed, with other symptoms, is frequently seen — not treated! The sense of helplessness which this propensity in a patient choked by his great possessions can arouse in a therapist is great. Two of my former patients come to mind. One, whose annual income was over a million dollars, was brought by relatives for treatment after he had made an attempt at suicide. Life, he said, no longer held anything of interest for him. "And I haven't the slightest idea," he said, "what to do with all my money. I don't need it, but I can't bear to give any away."

"So you decide to kill yourself," I asked, "in order to get away from it?"

"Well, what else can I do?" he replied weakly.

"Could you establish a memorial to your beloved father, endowing certain art forms in the smaller cities over the country, all named for him?"

"Oh," he said, brightening, "that would be wonderful! He would have loved that. Sure, I could do it, easily. I would enjoy it. It would honor him, well, both of us, forever. Let me think about it. I might just do that."

But he didn't. He didn't do anything. He existed for a few more years, then died, prematurely, to the satisfaction of his heirs and business associates who were not yet in his predicament, although they suffered from the same "disease."

I remember another patient who would become very angry when approached by anyone for a contribution to a cause.

"Why should I give what I have to others?" he demanded. "It's mine. I'm no socialist. I earned this — some of it — and I'm keeping it, not sharing it. It is mine, I tell you."

"But," I reminded him, "you are very unhappy with it. And you are very lonely. You have no heirs. You could make many people happier, including yourself, by disbursing some of it. Why be Mr. Scrooge?"

But he, too, went away sorrowing, for he, too, had great possessions. That was twenty years ago. He is still an unhappy Scrooge, still "in treatment" with one of my colleagues for the relief of all sorts of symptoms other than greed.

---

done, we know; tares are being sown in the wheat field at night. But is no one responsible, no one answerable for these acts? Anxiety and depression we all acknowledge, and even vague guilt feelings; but has no one committed any sins?

Where, indeed, did sin go? What became of it?

Lt. William Calley was portrayed to the world as a bloody villain, in both the English and American senses of that adjective. He slaughtered helpless women and babies with the hypocritical justification that they might be carrying concealed explosives. He was formally accused and tried for military disobedience as well as murder before a jury of peers who had been engaged in the same business of military destruction, and he was found guilty.

But a great cry went up from the people. Many sectors of the general public angrily disputed the possibility that what Calley did could be properly labeled a crime. Indeed, many would not concede that he even committed a sin or made a mistake. He had obeyed orders (they said); he had done what everyone wanted done or was doing, and it was for the sake of a great righteousness. Some might (and did) find him technically guilty of a crime, but what he did was right; it was no sin. It was a glorious, patriotic deed.

The Sixth Commandment, "Thou shalt not kill," obviously made a tacit exception of bullocks, lambs, Indians, Philistines, and Viet Cong. Every slayer can find reasons for making his particular violation an exception, a non-crime if not a non-sin. Hitler had his reasons for killing the Jews. Custer had his reasons for killing the Sioux. Our military men had reasons for killing Viet Cong soldiers, and the Viet Cong had their reasons for killing ours. Under certain circumstances purposive killing is frequently declared, by one side or another, to be a non-crime. But is it ever a non-sin? Or, is nothing now a sin?

Avoidance of the Word

The very word "sin," which seems to have disappeared, was a proud word. It was once a strong word, an ominous and serious word. It described a central point in every civilized human being's life plan and life style. But the word went away. It has almost disappeared — the word, along with the notion. Why? Doesn't anyone sin anymore? Doesn't anyone believe in sin?...

What Do You Mean By "Sin"?

"Now, Dr. Karl. You ought to define that word. What do you mean by 'sin'?" All kinds of things have been called sin in times past. It has been used as a scarehead for controlling the ignorant for centuries. But just what have you in mind? What kind of sin do you mean? Carnal sin? Mortal sin? Venial sin? Original sin? Existential sin?"

I could counter with, "What *was* the sin that no longer exists?" I mean any kind of wrongdoing that *we* used to call sin. I have in mind behavior that violates the moral code or the individual conscience or both; behavior which pains or harms or destroys my neighbor — or me, myself. You know, and *Time* knows — what wrongdoing is, and if a better word than sin is available, use it....

I believe there is "sin" which is expressed in ways which cannot be subsumed under verbal artifacts such as "crime," "disease," "delinquency," "deviancy." There *is* immorality; there *is* unethical behavior; there *is* wrongdoing. And I hope to show that there is usefulness in retaining the concept, and indeed the word, SIN, which now shows some signs of returning to public acceptance. I would like to help this trend along....

My proposal is for the revival or reassertion of personal responsibility in all human acts, good and bad. Not total responsibility, but not zero either. I believe that all evildoing in which we become involved to any degreee tends to evoke guilt feelings and depression. These may or may not be clearly perceived, but they affect us. They may be reacted to and covered up by all kinds of escapism, rationalization, and reaction or symptom formation. To revive the half-submerged idea of personal responsiblity and to seek appropriate measures of reparation might turn the tide of our aggressions and of the moral struggle in which much of the world population is engaged.

We will see our world dilemmas more and more as expressing *internal* personal moral problems instead of seeing them only as *external*, social, legal, or environmental complexities.

SPORTS AND RELIGION

Cornish Rogers

Mr. Rogers is an associate editor of **The Christian Century** and a minister in the United Methodist Church.

Bring the following questions to your reading:

1. What historical evidence does the author present to link sports and religion?
2. Do you agree with the author's association of politics and religion?
3. How does the author relate religion to football? Does he make a strong case?

Cornish Rogers, ''Sports, Religion and Politics: The Renewal of an Alliance,'' **The Christian Century**, April 5, 1972, pp. 392-94. Copyright 1972 Christian Century Foundation. Reprinted from the April 5, 1972 issue of **The Christian Century**.

No one in America who is interested in both sports and religion can overlook the unmistakable link between them — and that link is by no means limited to the fact that the lessons of sports lend themselves readily to analogies concerning godly living. Whether athletic events involve interschool rivalry or competition between the teams of two cities, the spectators tacitly infer that the contest represents the symbolic acting-out of a larger cosmic drama, and that the winner is somehow more virtuous than the loser, or at least more pleasing to the gods....

The Ancient Ties

It is clear, then, that the more closely we analyze the mystique of sports, psychologically and functionally, the more we tend to use religious language to describe it. And no wonder: from its beginnings, athletics was regarded as a religious cult and as a preparation for life. According to Rabbi Rudolph Brasch, ''Its roots were in man's desire to gain victory over foes seen and unseen, to influence the forces of nature, and to promote fertility among his crops and cattle.''

The word ''sport'' itself is an abbreviation, the shortened form of *disport* — an amusement or diversion. It is a derivative of the Latin *des-porto*, which literally means ''carry away.'' But though the enjoyment of sports has often diverted people from day-to-day cares and anxieties and carried them away to a world of excitement and thrills, sports began as a necessity for primal man's survival. In addition to fulfilling his innate desire for competition, sports enabled primitive man to develop the muscular strength and alertness to defend himself against human, animal and other natural foes.

But primitive man perceived his greatest enemies not as natural but as supernatural. The Zuni Indians in Mexico played games which they believed would magically bring rain to their drought-filled land and thus enable their crops to grow. Wrestling bouts in southern Nigeria were designed to encourage the growth of crops by sympathetic magic. Many games were held in the winter in order to hasten the return of spring and to ensure a fruitful season. And during the fall, at the end of the harvest season, an Eskimo tribe played a cup-and-ball game to ''catch the sun'' and thus delay its departure. "Playing the game," says Rabbi Brasch, was man's way to assure the "revival of nature and the victory of vegetation."

The association of sports with religion during the classical period is exemplified by the Olympic games, played in honor of Zeus, and the Pythian games, which were related to the oracles of Apollo and his shrine at Delphi. Such competitions were intended not only to honor the gods but also to celebrate peace and were in fact regarded as exercises in holiness. E. Norman Gardiner, in his book **Athletics of the Ancient World**, indicates that some of the events were funeral games conducted in honor of some soldier slain in battle. (And even the apostle Paul, though he rejected the pagan religious implications of the games, employed athletic metaphors in speaking of the faith — the early Christian wrestled with the powers of darkness, fought the good fight, and finished the race.)

The Sports Mystique and Politics

That politics should intrude into the relationship between sports and religion is readily understandable when it is remembered that many ancient rulers (like some present ones) also served as heads of the state religious establishment and in some cases were themselves considered at least semidivine. Thus sports have become a valuable political device for political leaders to use in consolidating — and even sacralizing — their power. When Richard Nixon awarded the University of Nebraska football team the title as national champions, he was courting for himself the mystique of a "divine king." And in this presidential year, he is not alone: a few weeks ago during the Florida primary race John Lindsay threw out the first baseball in a New York Yankees preseason game. No doubt other presidential aspirants will seek in some way to appropriate the sports mystique in the coming months.

Each of the serious candidates knows that, by whatever name it is called, America's "civil religion" is a vital force to be reckoned with. They recognize that Richard Nixon, by holding "nondenominational" Sunday services in the White House, has tried to co-opt for himself the symbolic embodiment of the undefined but pervasive religious consciousness that has character-ized our public life since the founding of the nation. He

DUNAGIN'S PEOPLE by Ralph Dunagin
Courtesy of Field Newspaper Syndicate

has sought to make more explicit the ''American Shinto'' by giving it a more pronounced shape and by according it an honored place in his presidency. Billy Graham, the foremost apostle of American evangelical nondenominationalism, has been installed as high priest. Recently one U.S. denominational leader, taking note of this trend, complained that there seems to be a stronger movement toward nondenominational religion than toward ecumenical religion.

Religion In the Football Stadium

In a manner comparable to the classical period of the Olympic games, the public festivals of America's civil religion are often held in the midst of massive sporting events. Anyone who watched televised football games last fall and winter can attest to the ''religious'' nature of the spectacle.

Several of last winter's games were dedicated to the late coach of the Green Bay Packers, Vince Lombardi, who seems to have earned a place in the panoply of the saints in American civil religion for his fierce discipline and his straightforward philosophy of play: ''Winning is the only thing.''

Football's halftime ceremonies often deal with patriotic themes. Through ingenious patterns on the playing field marching bands and prancing semi-nude girls form massive representations of the American flag. Meanwhile, overhead, U.S. air force planes fly intricate, close formations. Over the loudspeaker come appeals for the freeing of U.S. prisoners of war in Vietnam, and moments of silence are observed for those slain in the war. On occasion the restless television camera spies the President himself, enjoying the proceedings from a box seat.

The games are usually opened with prayer by a clergyman (it doesn't seem to matter whether the invoker is Protestant, Catholic or Jew), who offers prayer before the hushed thousands in the stadium, shamelessly linking God, country and good sportsmanship in his intercessions. The players as well as the spectators stand in respectful and reverent silence, though occasionally the television camera pans to a distracted athlete tugging at a private part of his anatomy or to a player chatting amiable with a colleague or vigorously chewing gum. To be sure, before leaving the dressing room, most teams have already had their ''devotions,'' led by one of the players, probably a member of the Fellowship of Christian Athletes.

It is perhaps because religious fervor is such a powerful physical stimulant that American athletics has developed its own religion. The essence of that religion is embodied in the Fellowship of Christian Athletes, a nationwide network of active and former college and professional athletes who meet together to witness to their faith — usually a personal pietistic, triumphalist faith — and to provide worship leadership to all professional teams, especially on Sunday mornings when the teams are on the road. Aggressively nondenominational, the group seeks to instill in young people a sense of the relationship between competitive sports and the struggle to maintain a Christian life. Its members preach that disciplines developed in sports provide a solid foundation for successful and holy living; they testify that their Christian faith has stood them in good stead on the athletic field.

Several leaders of the Fellowship of Christian Athletes have gone on to become public relations directors for commercial enterprises; some of the more able have landed political patronage jobs in conservative administrations for which they direct "physical fitness" programs. But the athletes of the fellowship make their most significant contribution in personifying what it means to be dedicated and successful adherents of American civil religion. And buttressed by the examples of those paragons, sports are rapidly becoming the dominant ritualistic expression of the reification of established religion in America.

AMERICA'S CIVIL RELIGION

Robert N. Bellah

Robert N. Bellah is Ford Professor of Sociology
and Comparative Studies at the University of Cali-
fornia, Berkeley. He is author of **Beyond Belief:
Essays on Religion in a Post-Traditional World**,
Tokugawa Religion, and most recently **The Broken
Covenant**. He is also the co-editor of **Religion in
America**.

As you read try to answer the following questions:

1. What does the author mean by the term ''civil
   religion''?
2. How does America's civil religion relate to
   Christianity?
3. What did the Civil War contribute to America's civil
   religion? What role does Abraham Lincoln play?
4. How does the author relate America's civil religion
   to its role in the world?
5. What does the author see as the ''third time of trial''
   for America's civil religion?

Robert N. Bellah, ''Civil Religion In America,'' **Daedalus**, Winter
1967, pp. 1-21. Reprinted by permission of **Daedalus**, Journal of The
American Academy of Arts and Sciences, Boston, Massachusetts.
Winter 1967, Religion In America.

While some have argued that Christianity is the national faith, and others that church and synagogue celebrate only the generalized religion of "the American Way of life," few have realized that there actually exists alongside of and rather clearly differentiated from the churches an elaborate and well-institutionalized civil religion in America. This article argues not only that there is such a thing, but also that this religion — or perhaps better, this religious dimension — has its own seriousness and integrity and requires the same care in understanding that any other religion does.[1]...

The words and acts of the founding fathers, especially the first few presidents, shaped the form and tone of the civil religion as it has been maintained ever since. Though much is selectively derived from Christianity, this religion is clearly not itself Christianity. For one thing, neither Washington nor Adams nor Jefferson mentions Christ in his inaugural address; nor do any of the subsequent presidents, although not one of them fails to mention God.[2] The God of the civil religion is not only rather "unitarian," he is also on the austere side, much more related to order, law, and right than to salvation and love. Even though he is somewhat deist in cast, he is by no means simply a watchmaker God. He is actively interested and involved in history, with a special concern for America. Here the analogy has much less to do with natural law than with ancient Israel; the equation of America with Israel in the idea of the "American Israel" is not infrequent.[3] What was implicit in the words of Washington... becomes explicit in Jefferson's second inaugural when he said: "I shall need, too, the favor of that Being in whose hands we are, who led our fathers, as Israel of old, from their native land and planted them in a country flowing with all the necessaries and comforts of life." Europe is Egypt; America, the promised land. God has led his people to establish a new sort of social order that shall be a light unto all the nations.[4]...

What we have, then, from the earliest years of the republic is a collection of beliefs, symbols, and rituals with respect to sacred things and institutionalized in a collectivity. This religion — there seems no other word for it — while not antithetical to and indeed sharing much in common with Christianity, was neither sectarian nor in any specific sense Christian. At a time when the society was overwhelmingly Christian, it seems unlikely that this lack of Christian reference was meant to spare the feelings of the tiny non-Christian minority. Rather, the civil religion expressed what those who set the precedents felt was appropriate under the circumstances. It reflected their private as well as public views. Nor was the civil religion simply "religion in general." While generality was undoubtedly seen as a virtue by some,...the civil religion was specific enough when it came to the topic of America. Precisely because of this specificity, the civil religion was saved from empty formalism and served as a genuine vehicle of national religious self-understanding....

> **There actually exists alongside of and rather clearly differentiated from the churches an elaborate and well-institutionalized civil religion in America.**

Civil War and Civil Religion

Until the Civil War, the American civil religion focused above all on the event of the Revolution, which was seen as the final act of the Exodus from the old lands across the waters. The Declaration of Independence and the Constitution were the sacred scriptures and Washington the divinely appointed Moses who led his people out of the hands of tyranny. The Civil War, which Sidney Mead calls "the center of American history," [5] was the second great event that involved the national self-understanding so deeply as to require expression in the civil religion. In 1835, Tocqueville wrote that the American republic had never really been tried, that victory in the Revolutionary War was more the result of British pre-occupation elsewhere and the presence of a powerful ally than of any great military success of the Americans....

With the Civil War, a new theme of death, sacrifice, and rebirth enters the civil religion. It is symbolized in the life and death of Lincoln. Nowhere is it stated more vividly than in the Gettysburg Address, itself part of the Lincolnian "New Testament" among the civil scriptures. Robert Lowell has recently pointed out the "insistent use of birth images" in this speech explicitly devoted to "these honored dead": "brought forth," "conceived," "created," "a new birth of freedom." He goes on to say:

> The Gettysburg Address is a symbolic and sacramental act. Its verbal quality is resonance combined with a logical, matter of fact, prosaic brevity.... In his words, Lincoln symbolically died, just as the Union soldiers really died — and as he himself was soon really to die. By his words, he gave the field of battle a symbolic significance that it had lacked. For us and our country, he left Jefferson's ideals of freedom and equality joined to the Christian sacrificial act of death and rebirth. I believe this is a meaning that goes beyond sect or religion and beyond peace and war, and is now part of our lives as a challenge, obstacle and hope.[6]

Lowell is certainly right in pointing out the Christian quality of the symbolism here, but he is also right in quickly disavowing any sectarian implication. The earlier symbolism of the civil religion had been Hebraic without being in any specific sense Jewish. The Gettysburg symbolism ("...those who here gave their lives, that that nation might live") is Christian without having anything to do with the Christian church.

The symbolic equation of Lincoln with Jesus was made relatively early. Herndon, who had been Lincoln's law partner, wrote:

> For fifty years God rolled Abraham Lincoln through his fiery furnace. He did it to try Abraham and to purify him for his purposes. This made Mr. Lincoln humble, tender, forebearing, sympathetic to suffering, kind, sensitive, tolerant; broadening, deepening and widening his whole nature; making him the noblest and loveliest character since Jesus Christ.... I believe that Lincoln was God's chosen one.[7]...

The new symbolism soon found both physical and ritualistic expression. The great number of the war dead required the establishment of a number of national cemeteries. Of these, the Gettysburg National Cemetery, which Lincoln's famous address served to dedicate, has been overshadowed only by the Arlington

National Cemetery. Begun somewhat vindictively on the Lee estate across the river from Washington, partly with the end that the Lee family could never reclaim it,[8] it has subsequently become the most hallowed monument of the civil religion....

Memorial Day, which grew out of the Civil War, gave ritual expression to the themes we have been discussing. As Lloyd Warner has so brilliantly analyzed it, the Memorial Day observance, especially in the towns and smaller cities of America, is a major event for the whole community involving a rededication to the martyred dead, to the spirit of sacrifice, and to the American vision.[9] Just as Thanksgiving Day, which incidentally was securely institutionalized as an annual national holiday only under the presidency of Lincoln, serves to integrate the family into the civil religion, so Memorial Day has acted to integrate the local community into the national cult. Together with the less overtly religious Fourth of July and the more minor celebrations of Veterans Day and the birthdays of Washington and Lincoln, these two holidays provide an annual ritual calendar for the civil religion. The public-school system serves as a particularly important context for the cultic celebration of the civil rituals....

The American civil religion was never anticlerical or militantly secular. On the contrary, it borrowed selectively from the religious tradition in such a way that the average American saw no conflict between the two. In this way, the civil religion was able to build up without any bitter struggle with the church powerful symbols of national solidarity and to mobilize deep levels of personal motivation for the attainment of national goals.

Such an achievement is by no means to be taken for granted. It would seem that the problem of a civil religion is quite general in modern societies and that the way it is solved or not solved will have repercussions in many spheres. One needs only to think of France to see how differently things can go. The French Revolution was anticlerical to the core and attempted to set up an anti-Christian civil religion. Throughout modern French history, the chasm between traditional Catholic symbols and the symbolism of 1789 has been immense....

The civil religion has not always been invoked in favor of worthy causes. On the domestic scene, an American-Legion type of ideology that fuses God, country, and flag has been used to attack nonconformist and liberal ideas and groups of all kinds. Still, it has been difficult to use the words of Jefferson and Lincoln to support special interests and undermine personal freedom. The defenders of slavery before the Civil War came to reject the thinking of the Declaration of Independence. Some of the most consistent of them turned against not only Jeffersonian democracy but Reformation religion; they dreamed of a South dominated by medieval chivalry and divine-right monarchy. [10] For all the overt religiosity of the radical right today, their relation to the civil religious consensus is tenuous, as when the John Birch Society attacks the central American symbol of Democracy itself.

GRAHAM-NIXON RELIGION IS PASSING AWAY

That American civic religion — religion represented by Billy Graham and President Nixon — is undergoing a massive revolution should not be surprising in a day when revolution is being urged in all areas of national life. If, as enlightened Americans agree, the older culture on which the Graham-Nixon kind of religion is based is passing away, a new civic religion will inevitably develop. Even if one does not accept the extravagant predictions of Charles Reich, it does indeed seem probable that the gospel of unquestioning patriotism, of the pursuit of economic success, of self-control and self-denial for the sake of one's future career and of puritanism with regard to personal morality will never again be taken as seriously in America as it once was.

James Hitchcock, "Religion and American Culture — The Next Phase," **The Christian Century,** September 20, 1972.

With respect to America's role in the world, the dangers of distortion are greater and the built-in safeguards of the tradition weaker. The theme of the American Israel was used, almost from the beginning, as a justification for the shameful treatment of the Indians so characteristic of our history. It can be overtly or implicitly linked to the idea of manifest destiny which has been used to legitimate several adventures in imperialism since the early-nineteenth century. Never has the danger been greater than today. The issue is not so much one of imperial expansion, of which we are accused, as of the tendency to assimilate all governments or parties in the world which support our immediate policies or call upon our help by invoking the notion of free institutions and democratic values. Those nations that are for the moment "on our side" become "the free world." A repressive and unstable military dictatorship in South Viet-Nam becomes "the free people of South Viet-Nam and their government." It is then part of the role of America as the New Jerusalem and "the last best hope on earth" to defend such governments with treasure and eventually with blood. When our soldiers are actually dying, it becomes possible to consecrate the struggle further by invoking the great theme of sacrifice....

The Third Time of Trial

In conclusion it may be worthwhile to relate the civil religion to the most serious situation that we as Americans now face, what I call the third time of trial. The first time of trial had to do with the question of independence, whether we should or could run our own affairs in our own way. The second time of trial was over the issue of slavery, which in turn was only the most salient aspect of the more general problem of the full institutionalization of democracy within our country. This second problem we are still far from solving though we have some notable successes to our credit. But we have been overtaken by a third great problem which has led to a third great crisis, in the midst of which we stand. This is the problem of responsible action in a revolutionary world, a world seeking to attain many of the things, material and spiritual, that we have already attained....

Out of the first and second times of trial have come,

177

as we have seen, the major symbols of the American civil religion. There seems little doubt that a successful negotiation of this third time of trial — the attainment of some kind of viable and coherent world order — would precipitate a major new set of symbolic forms. So far the flickering flame of the United Nations burns too low to be the focus of a cult, but the emergence of a genuine transnational sovereignty would certainly change this. It would necessitate the incorporation of vital international symbolism into our civil religion, or, perhaps a better way of putting it, it would result in American civil religion becoming simply one part of a new civil religion of the world....

Behind the civil religion at every point lie Biblical archetypes: Exodus, Chosen People, Promised Land, New Jerusalem, Sacrifical Death and Rebirth. But it is also genuinely American and genuinely new. It has its own prophets and its own martyrs, its own sacred events and sacred places, its own solemn rituals and symbols. It is concerned that America be a society as perfectly in accord with the will of God as men can make it, and a light to all the nations.

It has often been used and is being used today as a cloak for petty interests and ugly passions. It is in need — as is any living faith — of continual reformation, of being measured by universal standards. But it is not evident that it is incapable of growth and new insight.

It does not make any decision for us. It does not remove us from moral ambiguity, from being, in Lincoln's fine phrase, an "almost chosen people." But it is a heritage of moral and religious experience from which we still have much to learn as we formulate the decisions that lie ahead.

FOOTNOTES

1 Why something so obvious should have escaped serious analytical attention is in itself an interesting problem. Part of the reason is probably the controversial nature of the subject. From the earliest years of the nineteenth century, conservative religious and political groups have argued that Christianity is, in fact, the national religion. Some of them have from time to time and as recently as the 1950's proposed constitutional amendments that would explicitly recognize the sovereignty of Christ. In defending the doctrine of separation of church and state, opponents of such groups have denied that the national policy has,

intrinsically, anything to do with religion at all. The moderates on this issue have insisted that the American state has taken a permissive and indeed supportive attitude toward religious groups (tax exemption, et cetera), thus favoring religion but still missing the positive institutionalization with which I am concerned. But part of the reason this issue has been left in obscurity is certainly due to the peculiarly Western concept of "religion" as denoting a single type of collectivity of which an individual can be a member of one and only one at a time. The Durkeimian notion that every group has a religious dimension, which would be seen as obvious in southern or eastern Asia, is foreign to us. This obscures the recognition of such dimensions in our society.

2 God is mentioned or referred to in all inaugural addresses but Washington's second, which is a very brief (two paragraphs) and perfunctory acknowledgment. It is not without interest that the actual word **God** does not appear until Monroe's second inaugural, 5 March 1821. In his first inaugural, Washington refers to God as "that Almighty Being who rules the universe," "Great Author of every public and private good," "Invisible Hand," and "benign Parent of the Human Race." John Adams refers to God as "Providence," "Being who is supreme over all," "Patron of Order," "Foundation of Justice," and "Protector in all ages of the world of virtuous liberty." Jefferson speaks of "that Infinite Power which rules the destinies of the universe," and "that Being in whose hands we are." Madison speaks of "that Almighty Being whose power regulates the destiny of nations," and "Heaven." Monroe uses "Providence" and "the Almighty" in his first inaugural and finally "Almighty God" in his second. See **Inaugural Addresses of the Presidents of the United States from George Washington 1789 to Harry S. Truman 1949,** 82nd Congress, 2d Session, House Document No. 540, 1952.

3 For example, Abiel Abbot, pastor of the First Church in Haverhill, Massachusetts, delivered a Thanksgiving sermon in 1790, **Traits of Resemblance in the People of the United States of America to Ancient Israel**, in which he said, "It has been often remarked that the people of the United States come nearer to a parallel with Ancient Israel, than any other nation upon the globe. Hence 'Our American Israel' is a term frequently used; and common consent allows it apt and proper." Cited in Hans Kohn, **The Idea of Nationalism** (New York, 1961), p. 665.

4 That the Mosaic analogy was present in the minds of leaders at the very moment of the birth of the republic is indicated in the designs proposed by Franklin and Jefferson for a seal of the United States of America. Together with Adams, they formed a committee of three delegated by the Continental Congress on July 4, 1776, to draw up the new device. "Franklin proposed as the device Moses lifting up his wand and dividing the Red Sea while Pharaoh was overwhelmed by its waters, with the motto 'Rebellion to tyrants is obedience to God.' Jefferson proposed the children of Israel in the wilderness 'led by a cloud by day and a pillar of fire at night.' " Anson Phelps Stokes, **Church and State in the United States**, Vol. I (New York, 1950), pp. 467-468.

5 Sidney Mead, **The Lively Experiment** (New York, 1963), p. 12.

6 Allan Nevins (ed.), **Lincoln and The Gettysburg Address** (Urbana, Ill., 1964) pp. 88-89.

7 Quoted in Sherwood Eddy, **The Kingdom of God and the American Dream** (New York, 1941), p. 162.

8 Karl Decker and Angus McSween, **Historic Arlington** (Washington, D.C., 1892), pp. 60-67.
9 How extensive the activity associated with Memorial Day can be is indicated by Warner: "The sacred symbolic behavior of Memorial Day, in which scores of the town's organizations are involved, is ordinarily divided into four periods. During the year separate rituals are held by many of the associations for their dead, and many of these activities are connected with later Memorial Day events. In the second phase, preparations are made during the last three or four weeks for the ceremony itself, and some of the associations perform public rituals. The third phase consists of scores of rituals held in all the cemeteries, churches, and halls of the associations. These rituals consist of speeches and highly ritualized behavior. They last for two days and are climaxed by the fourth and last phase, in which all the separate celebrants gather in the center of the business district on the afternoon of Memorial Day. The separate organizations, with their members in uniform or with fitting insignia, march through the town, visit the shrines and monuments of the hero dead, and, finally enter the cemetery. Here dozens of ceremonies are held, most of them highly symbolic and formalized." During these various ceremonies Lincoln is continually referred to and the Gettysburg Address recited many times. W. Lloyd Warner, **American Life** (Chicago, 1962), pp. 8-9.
10 See Louis Hartz, "The Feudal Dream of the South," Part 4, **The Liberal Tradition in America** (New York, 1955).

DETERMINING SIN

Drawing by Dana Fradon; © 1975 The New Yorker Magazine, Inc.

'Miss Dugan, will you send someone in here who can distinguish right from wrong?'

Dr. Menninger, in reading nineteen, defined sin in general terms as

behavior that violates the moral code or the individual conscience or both; behavior which pains or harms or destroys my neighbor — or me, myself.

Using Dr. Menninger's definition, examine the following actions. Consider each action carefully. Mark

181

VS for actions you feel are very sinful. Mark **SF** for actions you feel are slightly sinful. Mark **NS** for actions you feel are not sinful. Then discuss and compare your judgments with those of other class members. Be able to present reasons for your judgments. Also, decide which two actions you believe are most sinful and the two that are least sinful. Again, be able to defend your choices.

VS = VERY SINFUL
SF = SLIGHTLY SINFUL
NS = NOT SINFUL

_____ 1. Using violence to achieve valuable goals

_____ 2. Obeying a superior's orders to execute unarmed civilians in a war situation

_____ 3. Getting an abortion

_____ 4. Failing to aid an injured pedestrian lying by the side of the road

_____ 5. Stealing a small item from a large company

_____ 6. Living as man and wife when not married

_____ 7. Sexual relations between consenting homosexuals

_____ 8. Collecting welfare when able to work

_____ 9. Lying

_____ 10. Stealing from a neighbor

_____ 11. Pretending to love someone to have sexual relations with that person

_____ 12. Selling dope to help support your family

_____ 13. Getting drunk frequently

_____ 14. Buying something with the intention of not paying the bill

_____ 15. Using drugs

6 CHAPTER

WHAT IS PATROITISM?

Readings
22. **What's Happened to Patriotism?**
    Max Rafferty
23. **Who Is Loyal to America?**
    Henry Steele Commager
24. **The Pragmatics of Patriotism**
    Robert A. Heinlein
25. **We Need a New Kind of Patriotism**
    Ralph Nader

WHAT'S HAPPENED TO PATRIOTISM?

Max Rafferty

This reading is a condensation of a speech for which the Freedoms Foundation at Valley Forge awarded the George Washington Honor Medal to the author.

Dr. Max Rafferty is Dean of the School of Education at Troy State University in Alabama. He formerly served as the Superintendent of Public Instruction for the state of California from 1963 until 1971. He has authored several books, including **What They Are Doing to Your Children**, **Max Rafferty on Education** and **Classroom Countdown**.

Reflect on the following questions while you read:

1. Why does the author claim the American patriot is a vanishing species?
2. What two things should America's schools have taught in the last twenty years that they neglected, in the author's opinion?
3. Why does Dr. Rafferty feel American schools are to blame for the decline in patriotism? Do you agree?

Max Rafferty, ''The Passing of the Patriot,'' reprinted with the author's permission.

Our Country, Right or Wrong!

I want to talk to you about a vanishing species — the American patriot. I hope to show you what you and I have done...to make possible — nay, to render inevitable — this dwindling decline of a once noble breed. And, at the end, I shall propose to you a simple question: "Is this what we want?"

First, go back with me in time.... Our country is in a strange sort of undeclared war against the forces of despotism, then as now. A young man volunteers to go behind the enemy lines to collect information. He is captured and tried as a spy and publicly questioned. Surrounded by the jeering foe, cut off beyond all hope of rescue, the rope already knotted around his bared throat and the pallor of approaching death already on his cheek, he breaks his steadfast silence. With the wind of another world cold upon his forehead, he speaks one short sentence, and his words echo down the corridors of time to us today, ringing and lighthearted and magnificent: "I only regret that I have but one life to give for my country."

His statue, with the throat still bared, stands today gazing with blind stone eyes across the green park in New York City, where I saw it not too long ago. He was a schoolmaster — God rest his soul — and he did not live to see his twenty-second birthday.

What were those blind eyes looking for a few years ago, I wonder, when for the first time in our history a substantial number of young men sold out their fellow American soldiers, and licked the boots of brutal Chinese and North Korean invaders, and made tape recordings praising Communism? What do those stone ears make of the other young men and women who seem to spend every waking moment agitating against ROTC, booing authorized Congressional committees, and parading in support of Fidel Castro?

Whether we like it or not, ladies and gentlemen, this is our doing — yours and mine. For the past twenty years, the great mistake has been made by my profession, and by the voters and taxpayers who permitted it.

This sizable minority of spineless, luxury-loving,

spiritless characters came right out of our classrooms. They played in our kindergartens, went on field trips to the bakery, and studied things called "social living" and "language arts" in our junior high schools. They were "adjusted to their peer groups." They were taught that competition was bad. They were told little about modern democratic capitalism. They were persuaded that the world was very shortly to become one big, happy family. They were taught to be kind, and democratic, and peaceful.

These last are praiseworthy goals. What went wrong?

There were two things, you see, that we *didn't* teach them. And oh! how they needed to learn these.

One was that most of the inhabitants of this big, bad-tempered, battling planet hate our American insides. This is hard to teach, and unpleasant to learn. It is the simple truth, nevertheless.

The other should have been simpler. It was to teach the children the real meaning of Decatur's great toast: "Our country! In her intercourse with foreign nations, may she always be right, but our country, right or wrong!"

Had they been taught these things, they would not now be wondering what all the fuss is about. They would know that their country was in danger, and that would be enough. It was enough in 1898, and 1917, and 1941. It's not enough today. Too many of them neither know nor care.

> **I think that education has deliberately debunked the hero to make room for the jerk.**

It's our own fault. What will History have to say of my generation of educators — the generation of the '30s, the '40s, and the '50s? We were so busy educating for "life adjustment" that we forgot that the first duty of a nation's schools is to preserve that nation.

Words that America had treasured as a rich legacy, that had sounded like trumpet calls above the clash of arms and the fury of debate, we allowed to fade from the classrooms and the consciousness of the pupils. "Liberty and Union, now and forever, one and inseparable..." "We have met the enemy and they are ours..." "Millions for defense, but not one cent for tribute..."

Search for these towering phrases in vain today in too many of our schools, in the hearts and minds of too many of our children.... We have no further need of Websters — nor of Nathan Hales.

Our Schools Teach Trivia Not Patriotism

Our sin was greater than this, however. Patriotism feeds upon hero-worship, and we decided to abolish heroes. Even the fairy tales and nursery rhymes, beloved by generations of children, we pronounced too "violent" and "brutal" for the children to hear until after we had tinkered with them. Hansel and Gretel we neutralized to the status of children on a Sunday School picnic, and Jack the Giant-Killer to a schoolboy swatting flies. Everything that was fearful and wonderful, we leveled off to the lowest *common* denominator.

Ulysses and Penelope have been replaced by Dick and Jane in the textbooks of our schools. The quest of the Golden Fleece has been crowded out by the visit of Tom and Susan to the zoo. The deeds of the heroes before Troy are now passe, and the peregrinations of the local milkman as he wends his way among the stodgy streets and littered alleys of Blah City are deemed worthy of numberless pages in our readers. The sterile culture of the Pueblo Indians looms large in our curriculum, but the knightly Crusaders are glossed over. Bobby and Betty pursue their insipid goal of a ride in the district garbage truck with good old crotchety Mr. Jones, while the deathless ride of Paul Revere goes unwept, unhonored, and unsung. It is interesting and significant, I think, that education has deliberately debunked the hero to make room for the jerk.

Today's hero — if there is one — is fashioned in the blasphemous image of Ourselves.

187

He is "Daddy" in the second reader, who comes mincing home with his eternal briefcase from his meaningless day in his antiseptic office just in time to pat Jip the dog and carry blonde little Laurie into the inevitable white bungalow on his stylishly padded shoulders.

He is "Mommy" in the third grade books, always silk-stockinged and impeccable after a day spent over the electric range, with never a cross word on her carefully made-up lips and never an idea in her empty head.

He is all the insufferable nonentities who clutter up the pages our elementary textbooks with their vapid ditherings about humdrum affairs which could never be of conceivable interest to anybody....

When I think of the doors we've closed upon the children! The wonderful pantheon of youthful gods and goddesses that my generation knew and loved; the great parade of heroes who made old Earth a magic place for boys and girls!

Wilfred of Ivanhoe rode stirrup to stirrup with Richard the Lion-Hearted, and the evil hold of Torquilstone burned eternal witness to the power of youth and goodness. Laughing and shouting in the same great company rode Arthur with his Table Round, forever splintering their lances in the cause of Right. Roistering and invincible swaggered Porthos, Athos, and Aramis, with the young D'Artagnan, ever ready to draw those magic blades for truth and glory and the Queen....

The horn of Roland echoed through the pass at Roncevalles, and somehow caught and mingled in our memories with the far-off blast of Robin Hood, calling down the misty years upon his merry men of Sherwood.

Were not these fit heroes for the chidren?...

It remained for our generation to turn its back upon the heroes of the children. For Siegfried in the lair of Fafnir, we have substituted Muk-Muk the Eskimo Boy, and we have replaced Horatius at the Bridge with Little Pedro from Argentina.

Mark this. Until...a few years ago, most schools on all levels were teaching trivia. Today, too many —

especially on the elementary level — are still doing so.

If you doubt this, don't take my word for it. Visit classroom after classroom in widely separated regions of this country, as I have done.

AMERICANS MUST SACRIFICE

I want to propose just one large category of concept and activity which, I believe, is contributing to an attitude of hostility toward the American Dream. It is the spreading preoccupation, particularly among the youth, with one's own comfort, one's own physical gratification, one's right to do whatever he pleases as long as he doesn't significantly harm someone else, one's own security, one's own immediate desires, and the corollary belligerent intolerance of any laws, customs, or considerations for other people which might prevent me from doing my thing right now. Protest has become a way of life. If the individual's comfort and convenience are not at a maximum, then whatever is thwarting them should be attacked.

The government inaugurated in 1789 was committed to maximizing the dignity of all citizens. It recognized the eternal need for change in the governing process and the governing personnel and it created the mechanisms for orderly change. It guaranteed to all citizens certain privileges and devised a judiciary to try to assure that those privileges were fairly interpreted and properly maintained. However, in attending to all aspects of maximizing human dignity, the whole structure of the government was posited upon the requirement that the citizens, every citizen, would have to make some very great sacrifices. Each would have to pay duly levied taxes in order to sustain the authorized operations of the government. Each citizen would have to forego his other activities when called to jury duty. Each would submit peacefully to the will of the majority when it was expressed by vote, directing his own disappointments and dissatisfactions when thwarted by the majority vote, into legal and appropriate channels with the hope of subsequently making his own, the majority vote.

This form of government was entirely dependent upon a universal commitment to certain superior goals which necessitated personal sacrifices, acceptance of restrictions and conformity where the public weal was engaged. To achieve a new level of freedom for all, certain aspects of personal freedom had to be sacrificed by all.

Against this necessity for sacrifice, the current enthusiasm for total personal freedom, the current insistence upon exercising one's own whims with a disregard for the sensitivities of others, the quickening readiness to pronounce one's own particular objectives as uniquely moral and therefore beyond the purview of publicly established limits — all of these attitudes and actions stand in hostility to what this country is all about, and contribute to the disenchantment with America.

John Howard, "Patriotism Revisited," **Vital Speeches of the Day**, September 17, 1969, pp. 27-28. Reprinted with permission.

Watch the abler pupils grow dull and apathetic, bored and lackluster, as they yawn over Bill and Tom's Trip to the Farm, or Sally's Fun at the Orange Grove. Then, suddenly — as though opening an enchanted window upon a radiant pageant — give them the story of the wrath of Achilles. Let them stand with Casabianca upon the burning deck. Trek with them in spirit to the Yukon, and with glorious Buck let them answer the call of the wild. Place them upon the shot-swept shrouds of the Bonhomme Richard, and let them thrill to those words flashing like a rapier out of our past, "I have not yet begun to fight." Kneel with them behind the cotton bales at New Orleans with Andy Jackson at their side, as the redcoats begin to emerge from the Louisiana mists and the sullen guns of Lafitte begin to pound.

Watch their faces. See the eyes brighten and the spirits ruffle. See the color come, the backs straighten, the arms go up. They dream, they live, they glow. Patriotism will come easily to them now, as it does to all of us who know our nation's past — and love it.

Teach them the grand old songs. How long has it been since California children learned to sing "Columbia, the Gem of the Ocean"? And why was it dropped. Probably because someone decided that the lines which end, "The Army and Navy forever! Three cheers for the Red, White and Blue!" were hopelessly out of place in our brave new world of foreign aid and peaceful coexistence and collaboration.

I say that we had better thank God for the army and navy! And — with half the world at our throats — we had better teach our children that it is not a disgrace, but a priceless privilege, to wear our country's uniform!...

The results are plain for all to see: the worst of our youngsters growing up to become...Slobs, whose favorite sport is ravaging little girls and stomping polio victims to death; the best of our youth coming into maturity for all the world like young people fresh from a dizzying roller-coaster ride, with everything blurred, with nothing clear, with no positive standards, with everything in doubt. No wonder so many of them welsh out and squeal and turn traitor when confronted with the grim reality of Red military force and the crafty cunning of Red psychological warfare.

We as a people have been taunted and reviled and challenged in the last few years as we thought no one would ever challenge us. A soulless Thing slavers at us today on all the continents, under all the seas, and out into the void of interplanetary space itself — a rotten, hateful, vicious entity. Our national nose has been first tweaked and then rubbed contemptuously into the dirt. The flag for which our ancestors bled and died has been torn down and unspeakably defiled by a dozen little pipsqueak comic-opera countries emboldened by our spinelessness and encouraged by our sneering Enemy. I don't know when at long last the American people will rise in all the power and majesty of their great tradition to put an end to this role of international doormat which we have assumed of late, and which becomes us so poorly.

But I do know one thing. When that time comes — and it cannot be too far distant — we educators had better not be caught short. We had better not be caught withholding from the nation's children the wonderful, sharp-edged glittering sword of Patriotism.

What is the alternative? You see that all about you now, in all the headlines. Do you like it? As I said in the beginning, "Is this what we want?"

Or rather, do we want our young people informed and disciplined and alert — militant for freedom, clear-eyed to the filthy menace of Communist corruption? Do we want them happy in their love of country?

If your answer is "Yes," then go home and get busy. It is to this that I propose that we dedicate ourselves in the years to come. We have not an hour to spare. If Almighty God grants us the time and the will, we may still be able to preserve this lovely land of ours as it once was and — please God — will yet be again; a nation fit for heroes — serene in the knowledge of our past — confident and ready for whatever the future may bring — stretching in warmth of heart and unity of purpose "from sea to shining sea."

WHO IS LOYAL
TO AMERICA?

Henry Steele Commager

Henry Steele Commager is an educator and lecturer, and is currently a professor of history at Amherst College. He has earned many honors for his work in the United States and in other nations. He is the author of many books in the field of history, including **The Growth of the American Republic**, **The American Mind**, and **The Heritage of America**.

Consider the following questions while reading:

1. What does the author refer to with the term "the new loyalty"? ·
2. How does the author define "loyalty"?
3. In the author's opinion, who are those who are really disloyal in America?

Henry Steele Commager, "Who Is Loyal to America?" **Harpers**, September 1947, pp. 195-99. Reprinted with permission from the author.

The New Loyalty

What is the new loyalty? It is, above all, conformity. It is the uncritical and unquestioning acceptance of America as it is — the political institutions, the social relationships, the economic practices. It rejects inquiry into the race question or socialized medicine, or public housing, or into the wisdom or validity of our foreign policy. It regards as particularly heinous any challenge to what is called "the system of private enterprise," identifying that system with Americanism. It abandons evolution, repudiates the once popular concept of progress, and regards America as a finished product, perfect and complete.

It is, it must be added, easily satisfied. For it wants not intellectual conviction nor spiritual conquest, but mere outward conformity. In matters of loyalty it takes the word for the deed, the gesture for the principle. It is content with the flag salute, and does not pause to consider the warning of our Supreme Court that "a person gets from a symbol the meaning he puts into it, and what is one man's comfort and inspiration is another's jest and scorn." It is satisfied with membership in respectable organizations and, as it assumes that every member of a liberal organization is a Communist, concludes that every member of a conservative one is a true American. It has not yet learned that not everyone who saith Lord, Lord, shall enter into the kingdom of Heaven. It is designed neither to discover real disloyalty nor to foster true loyalty....

The concept of loyalty as conformity is a false one. It is narrow and restrictive, denies freedom of thought and of conscience, and is irremediably stained by private and selfish considerations. "Enlightened loyalty," wrote Josiah Royce, who made loyalty the very core of his philosophy,

> means harm to no man's loyalty. It is at war only with disloyalty, and its warfare, unless necessity constrains, is only a spiritual warfare. It does not foster class hatreds; it knows of nothing reasonable about race prejudices; and it regards all races of men as one in their need of loyalty. It ignores mutual misunderstandings. It loves its own wherever upon earth its own, namely loyalty itself, is to be found.

Justice, charity, wisdom, spirituality, he added, were all definable in terms of loyalty, and we may properly ask which of these qualities our contemporary champions of loyalty display.

Above all, loyalty must be to something larger than oneself, untainted by private purposes or selfish ends. But what are we to say of the attempts by the NAM and by individual corporations to identify loyalty with the system of private enterprise? Is it not as if officeholders should attempt to identify loyalty with their own party, their own political careers? Do not those corporations which pay for full-page advertisements associating Americanism with the competitive system expect, ultimately, to profit from that association? Do not those organizations that deplore, in the name of patriotism, the extension of government operation of hydroelectric power expect to profit from their campaign?

Certainly it is a gross perversion not only of the concept of loyalty but of the concept of Americanism to identify it with a particular economic system....

There is, it should be added, a further danger in the willful identification of Americanism with a particular body of economic practices....If Americanism is equated with competitive capitalism, what happens to it if competitive capitalism comes a cropper? If loyalty and private enterprise are inextricably associated, what is to preserve loyalty if private enterprise fails? Those who associate Americanism with a particular program of economic practices have a grave responsibility, for if their program should fail, they expose Americanism itself to disrepute.

The effort to equate loyalty with conformity is misguided because it assumes that there is a fixed content to loyalty and that this can be determined and defined. But loyalty is a principle, and eludes definition except in its own terms. It is devotion to the best interests of the commonwealth, and may require hostility to the particular policies which the government pursues, the particular practices which the economy undertakes, the particular institutions which society maintains. "If there is any fixed star in our Constitutional constellation," said the Supreme Court in the Barnette case, "it is that no official, high or petty, can prescribe what shall be orthodox in politics, nationalism, religion, or other matters of opinion, or force citizens to confess by

word or act their faith therein. If there are any circumstances which permit an exception they do not now
occur to us.''

True Loyalty

True loyalty may require, in fact, what appears to
the naive to be disloyalty. It may require hostility to
certain provisions of the Constitution itself, and historians have not concluded that those who subscribed to
the "Higher Law" were lacking in patriotism. We
should not forget that our tradition is one of protest and
revolt, and it is stultifying to celebrate the rebels of the
past — Jefferson and Paine, Emerson and Thoreau —
while we silence the rebels of the present. "We are a
rebellious nation," said Theodore Parker, known in his
day as the Great American Preacher, and went on:

> Our whole history is treason; our blood was attainted
> before we were born; our creeds are infidelity to the mother
> church; our constitution, treason to our fatherland. What of
> that? Though all the governors in the world bid us commit
> treason against man, and set the example, let us never
> submit.

Those who would impose upon us a new concept of
loyalty not only assume that this is possible, but have
the presumption to believe that they are competent to

THE CORE OF AMERICANISM

The most distinctively American philosophies
have been transcendentalism — which is the
philosophy of the Higher Law — and pragmatism
— which is the philosophy of experimentation and
pluralism. These two principles are the very core
of Americanism: the principle of the Higher Law,
or of obedience to the dictates of conscience rather
than of statues, and the principle of pragmatism,
or the rejection of a single good and of the notion
of a finished universe. From the beginning
Americans have known that there were new
worlds to conquer, new truths to be discovered.
Every effort to confine Americanism to a single
pattern, to constrain it to a single formula, is disloyalty to everything that is valid in Americanism.

196

write the definition. We are reminded of Whitman's defiance of the "never-ending audacity of elected persons." Who are those who would set the standards of loyalty? They are Rankins and Bilbos, officials of the D.A.R. and the Legion and the NAM, Hearsts and McCormicks. May we not say of Rankin's harangues on loyalty what Emerson said of Webster at the time of the Seventh of March speech: "The word honor in the mouth of Mr. Webster is like the word love in the mouth of a whore."

What do men know of loyalty who make a mockery of the Declaration of Independence and the Bill of Rights, whose energies are dedicated to stirring up race and class hatreds, who would straitjacket the American spirit? What indeed do they know of America — the America of Sam Adams and Tom Paine, of Jackson's defiance of the Court and Lincoln's celebration of labor, of Thoreau's essay on Civil Disobedience and Emerson's championship of John Brown, of the America of the Fourierists and the Come-Outers, of cranks and fanatics, of socialists and anarchists? Who among American heroes could meet their tests, who would be cleared by their committees? Not Washington, who was a rebel. Not Jefferson, who wrote that all men are created equal and whose motto was "rebellion to tyrants is obedience to God." Not Garrison, who publicly burned the Constitution; or Wendell Phillips, who spoke for the underprivileged everywhere and counted himself a philosophical anarchist; not Seward of the Higher Law or Sumner of racial equality. Not Lincoln, who admonished us to have malice toward none, charity for all; or Wilson, who warned that our flag was "a flag of liberty of opinion as well as of political liberty"; or Justice Holmes, who said that our Constitution is an experiment and that while that experiment is being made "we should be eternally vigilant against attempts to check the expression of opinions that we loathe and believe to be fraught with death."

There are further and more practical objections against the imposition of fixed concepts of loyalty or tests of disloyalty. The effort is itself a confession of fear, a declaration of insolvency. Those who are sure of themselves do not need reassurance, and those who have confidence in the strength and the virtue of America do not need to fear either criticism or competition. The effort is bound to miscarry. It will not apprehend those who are really disloyal, it will not even frighten them; it will affect only those who can be labeled "radical." It is sobering to recall that though the Japanese relocation program, carried through at such incalculable cost in misery and tragedy, was justified to us on the ground that the Japanese were potentially disloyal, the record does not disclose a single case of Japanese disloyalty or sabotage during the whole war....

Who Are Disloyal?

Who are those who are really disloyal? Those who inflame racial hatreds, who sow religious and class dissensions. Those who subvert the Constitution by violating the freedom of the ballot box. Those who make a mockery of majority rule by the use of the filibuster. Those who impair democracy by denying equal educational facilities. Those who frustrate justice by lynch law or by making a farce of jury trials. Those who deny freedom of speech and of the press and of assembly. Those who press for special favors against the interest of the commonwealth. Those who regard public office as a source of private gain. Those who would exalt the military over the civil. Those who for selfish and private purposes stir up national antagonisms and expose the world to the ruin of war....

If our democracy is to flourish it must have criticism, if our government is to function it must have dissent. Only totalitarian governments insist upon conformity and they — as we know — do so at their peril. Without criticism abuses will go unrebuked; without dissent our dynamic system will become static. The American people have a stake in the maintenance of the most thorough-going inquisition into American institutions. They have a stake in nonconformity, for they know that the American genius is nonconformist. They have a stake in experimentation of the most radical character, for they know that only those who prove all things can hold fast that which is good.

READING 24

THE PRAGMATICS OF PATRIOTISM

Robert A. Heinlein

Robert Heinlein is famous for his fiction. He is the author of over forty books, most of them dealing with science fiction and futuristics. Some of his books are **Stranger In A Strange Land**, **Beyond This Horizon** and **Green Hills of Earth**. He is a graduate of the U.S. Naval Academy and served in the Navy for nine years. The following reading was originally delivered as the James Forrestal Memorial Lecture to the Brigade of Midshipmen at the Naval Academy in 1973.

Consider the following questions while reading:

1. Why does the author think many American intellectuals sneer at patriotism?
2. How does the author define "moral behavior"?
3. Why does the author believe baboons exhibit moral behavior?
4. How do you think the author would react to the previous reading, Reading 23?

Robert A. Heinlein, "The Pragmatics of Patriotism," **Human Events**, January 26, 1974, pp. 84-85. © 1973 — Robert A. Heinlein. All rights reserved.

Leftist Sneers

Today, in the United States, it is popular among self-styled "intellectuals" to sneer at patriotism. They seem to think that it is axiomatic that any civilized man is a pacifist, and they treat the military profession with contempt. "Warmongers" — "Imperialists" — "Hired killers in uniform" — you have all heard such sneers and you will hear them again. One of their favorite quotations is: "Patriotism is the last refuge of a scoundrel."

What they never mention is that the man who made that sneering wisecrack was a fat, gluttonous slob who was pursued all his life by a pathological fear of death.

I propose to prove that a baboon on watch while his herd grazes is morally superior to that fat poltroon who made that wisecrack.

Patriotism is the most practical of all human characteristics.

But in the present decadent atmosphere patriots are often too shy to talk about it — as if it were something shameful or an irrational weakness.

But patriotism is not sentimental nonsense. Nor something dreamed up by demagogues. Patriotism is as necessary a part of man's evolutionary equipment as are his eyes, as useful to the race as eyes are to the individual.

A man who is *not* patriotic is an evolutionary dead end. This is not sentiment but the hardest sort of logic.

Fundamentals Cited

To prove that patriotism is a necessity we must go back to fundamentals. Take any breed of animal — for example, *tyrannosaurus rex*. What is the most basic thing about him? The answer is that *tyrannosaurus rex* is dead, gone, extinct.

Now take *homo sapiens*. The first fact about him is that he is not extinct, he is alive.

Which brings us to the second fundamental

question: Will *homo sapiens* stay alive? Will he survive?

We can answer part of that at once: Individually, *homo sapiens* will *not* survive. It is unlikely that anyone here tonight will be alive 80 years from now; it approaches mathematical certainty that we will all be dead a hundred years from now as even the youngest plebe here would be 118 years old then — if still alive.

Some men do live that long, but the percentage is so microscopic as not to matter. Recent advances in biology suggest that human life may be extended to a century and a quarter, even a century and a half — but this will create more problems than it solves. When a man reaches my age or thereabouts, the last great service he can perform is to die and get out of the way of younger people.

Very well, as individuals we all die. This brings us to the second half of the question: Does *homo sapiens as a breed* have to die? The answer is: No, it is *not* unavoidable.

We have two situations, mutually exclusive: Mankind surviving, and mankind extinct. With respect to morality, the second situation is a null class. An extinct breed has *no* behavior, moral or otherwise.

Since survival is the sine qua non, I now define ''moral behavior'' as ''behavior that tends toward survival.'' I won't argue with philosophers or theologians who choose to use the word ''moral'' to mean something else, but I do not think anyone can define ''behavior that tends toward extinction'' as being ''moral'' without stretching the word ''moral'' all out of shape.

We are now ready to observe the hierarchy of moral behavior from its lowest level to its highest.

The simplest form of moral behavior occurs when a man or other animal fights for his own survival. Do not belittle such behavior as being merely selfish. Of course it is selfish, but selfishness is the bedrock on which all moral behavior starts and it can be immoral only when it conflicts with a higher moral imperative.

> **Patriotism is the most practical of all human characteristics.**

An animal so poor in spirit that he won't even fight on his own behalf is already an evolutionary dead end; the best he can do for his breed is to crawl off and die, and not pass on his defective genes.

The next higher level is to work, fight, and sometimes die for your own immediate family. This is the level at which six pounds of mother cat can be so fierce that she'll drive off a police dog. It is the level at which a father takes a moonlighting job to keep his kids in college — and the level at which a mother or father dives into a flood to save a drowning child — and it is still moral behavior even when it fails.

Moral Behavior Tested

The next higher level is to work, fight, and sometimes die for a group larger than the unit family — an extended family, a herd, a tribe — and take another look at that baboon on watch; he's at that moral level. I don't think baboon language is complex enough to permit them to discuss such abstract notions as "morality" or "duty" or "loyalty" — but it is evident that baboons *do* operate morally and *do* exhibit the traits of duty and loyalty; we see them in action. Call it "instinct" if you like — but remember that assigning a name to a phenomenon does not explain it.

But that baboon behavior can be explained in evolutionary terms. Evolution is a process that never stops. Baboons who fail to exhibit moral behavior do not survive; they wind up as meat for leopards. Every baboon generation has to pass this examination in moral behavior; those who bilge it don't have progeny. Perhaps the old bull of the tribe gives lessons, but the leopard decides who graduates — and there is no appeal from his decision. We don't have to understand the details to observe the outcome: Baboons behave morally — for baboons.

The next level in moral behavior higher than that exhibited by the baboon is that in which duty and loyalty are shown toward a group of your own kind too large for an individual to know all of them. We have a name for that. It is called "patriotism."

Behaving on a still higher moral level were the astronauts who went to the Moon, for their actions tend toward the survival of the entire race of mankind. The door they opened leads to the hope that *homo sapiens* will survive indefinitely long, even longer than this solid planet on which we stand tonight. As a direct result of what they did, it is now possible that the human race will *never* die....

I must pause to brush off those parlor pacifists I mentioned earlier, for they contend that *their* actions are on this highest moral level. They want to put a stop to war; they say so. Their purpose is to save the human race from killing itself off; they say that, too. Anyone who disagrees with them must be a bloodthirsty scoundrel — and they'll tell you that to your face.

I won't waste time trying to judge their motives; my criticism is of their mental processes: Their heads aren't screwed on tight. They live in a world of fantasy.

Let me stipulate that, if the human race managed its affairs sensibly, we could do without war.

Yes — and if pigs had wings, they could fly.

I don't know what planet those pious pacifists are talking about, but it can't be the third one out from the Sun. Anyone who has seen the Far East — or Africa — or the Middle East — knows or certainly should know that there is *no* chance of abolishing war in the foreseeable future....

Examples of Heroism

Patriotism — moral behavior at the national level. *Non sibi sed Patria*. Nathan Hale's last words: "I regret that I have but one life to give for my country." Torpedo Squadron Eight making its suicidal attack. Four chaplains standing fast while the water rises around them. Thomas Jefferson saying, "The Tree of Liberty must be refreshed from time to time with the blood of patriots." A submarine skipper giving the order, "Take her *down*!" while he himself is still topside. Jonas Ingram standing on the steps of Bancroft Hall and shouting, "The Navy has no place for good losers! The Navy needs tough sons of bitches who can get out there and *win*!"

> **Patriotism — an abstract word used to describe a type of behavior as harshly practical as good brakes and good tires. It means that you place the welfare of your nation ahead of your own, even if it costs you your life.**

Men who go down to the sea in ships have long had another way of expressing the same moral behavior tagged by the abstract expression "patriotism." Spelled out in simple Anglo-Saxon words, "Patriotism" reads "Women and children first!"

And that is the moral result of realizing a self-evident biological fact: Men are expendable; women and children are not. A tribe or a nation can lose a high percentage of its men and still pick up the pieces and go on, as long as the women and children are saved. But if you fail to save the women and children, you've had it, you're done, you're *through*! You join *tyrannosaurus rex*, one more breed that bilged its final test....

Nevertheless, as a mathematical proposition in the facts of biology, children and women of child-bearing age are the ultimate treasure that we must save. Every human culture is based on "Women and children first" — and any attempt to do it any other way leads quickly to extinction.

Possibly extinction is the way we are headed. Great nations have died in the past; it can happen to us.

Nor am I certain how good our chances are. To me it seems self-evident that any nation that loses its patriotic fervor is on the skids. Without that indispensable survival factor the end is only a matter of time. I don't know how deeply the rot has penetrated — but it seems to me that there has been a change for the worse in the last 50 years. Possibly I am misled by the offensive behavior of a noisy but unimportant minority. But it does seem to me that patriotism has lost its grip on a large percentage of our people.

I hope I am wrong — because if my fears are well grounded, I would not bet two cents on this nation's chance of lasting even to the end of this century.

But there is no way to force patriotism on anyone. Passing a law will not create it, nor can we buy it by appropriating so many billions of dollars....

I said that ''patriotism'' is a way of saying ''Women and children first.'' And that no one can force a man to feel this way. Instead, he must embrace it freely. I want to tell about one such man. He wore no uniform and no one knows his name, nor where he came from; all we know is what he did.

> **Since survival is the sine qua non, I now define ''moral behavior'' as ''behavior that tends toward survival.''**

In my home town 60 years ago when I was a child, my mother and father used to take me and my brothers and sisters out to Swope Park on Sunday afternoons. It was a wonderful place for kids, with picnic grounds and lakes and a zoo. But a railroad line cut straight through it.

One Sunday afternoon a young married couple were crossing these tracks. She apparently did not watch her step, for she managed to catch her foot in the frog of a switch to a siding and could not pull it free. Her husband stopped to help her.

But try as they might they could not get her foot loose. While they were working at it, a tramp showed up, walking the ties. He joined the husband in trying to pull the young woman's foot loose. No luck.

Out of sight around the curve a train whistled. Perhaps there would have been time to run and flag it down, perhaps not. In any case both men went right ahead trying to pull her free — and the train hit them.

The wife was killed, the husband was mortally injured and died later, the tramp was killed — and testimony showed that neither man made the slightest effort to save himself.

The husband's behavior was heroic, but what we expect of a husband toward his wife: his right, and his proud privilege, to die for his woman. But what of this nameless stranger? Up to the very last second he could have jumped clear. He did not. He was still trying to save this woman he had never seen before in his life, right up to the very instant the train killed him. And that's all we'll ever know about him.

This is how a man dies.

This is how a *man*...lives!

WE NEED A NEW KIND OF PATRIOTISM

Ralph Nader

Ralph Nader is a lawyer in Washington, author and a world famous crusader for the U.S. consumer.

As you read consider the following questions:

1. Why was patriotism important during the early days of our country, in the author's opinion?
2. Why does he feel we now need a new kind of patriotism?
3. What four points does Mr. Nader suggest we use as guidelines in searching for a new kind of patriotism?

Ralph Nader, "We Need a New Kind of Patriotism," **The Saturday Evening Post**, July 1, 1971, pp. 4-5. Reprinted with permission from **The Saturday Evening Post** © 1971 The Curtis Publishing Company.

At a recent meeting of the national PTA, the ideal-ism and commitment of many young people to environ-mental and civil rights causes were being discussed. A midde-aged woman, who was listening closely, stood up and asked: ''But what can we do to make young people today patriotic?''

In a very direct way, she illuminated the tensions contained in the idea of patriotism. These tensions, which peak at moments of public contempt or respect for patriotic symbols such as the flag, have in the past few years divided the generations and pitted children against parents. Highly charged exchanges take place between those who believe that patriotism is auto-matically possessed by those in authority and those who assert that patriotism is not a pattern imposed but a condition earned by the quality of an individual's, or a people's, behavior. The struggle over symbols, epithets and generalities impedes a clearer understanding of the meaning and value of patriotism. It is time to talk of patriotism, not as an abstraction steeped in nostalgia, but as behavior that can be judged by the standard of ''liberty and justice for all.''

Patriotism can be a great asset for any organized society, but it can also be a tool manipulated by un-scrupulous or cowardly leaders and elites. The develop-ment of a sense of patriotism was a strong unifying force during our Revolution and its insecure aftermath. Defined then and now as ''love of country,'' patriotism was an extremely important motivating force with which to confront foreign threats to the young nation. It was no happenstance that *The Star Spangled Banner* was composed during the War of 1812 when the Red-coats were not only coming but already here. For a weak frontier country beset by the competitions and aggressions of European powers in the New World, the martial virtues were those of sheer survival. America produced patriots who never moved beyond the borders of their country. They were literally defenders of their home.

As the United States moved into the 20th century and became a world power, far-flung alliances and wars fought thousands of miles away stretched the boundaries of patriotism. ''Making the world safe for democracy'' was the grandiose way Woodrow Wilson put it. At other times and places (such as Latin America) it became distorted into ''jingoism.'' World

PATRIOTISM AND IDEALS

American patriotism has had to sustain itself on something different, and possibly less meaty, than love of place. Patriotism directed toward the American federation has based itself on ideals and institutions: ideals like independence, freedom, democracy, equality; institutions such as a government of limited powers, a system of checks and balances, trial by jury, the right to vote.

To the extent that these denials and institutions have been interpreted by all of us in the same way, we have had a consistent and sufficient "patriotism" or "loyalty." However, interpretations have been varied and, at times, most divisive. There is no semantic difficulty about the love of one's fatherland. The love is simply there. But ideals have to be expressed in words and sold as slogans. Does freedom mean freedom for black people too? Does equality imply equal sharing in this world's material goods? Does a system of checks and balances mean that the Supreme Court can throw out an act of Congress? Does the right to vote apply to females? These and other questions have shaken American patriotism badly on occasion.

James P. Speer, "On The Nature Of Patriotism," **The Christian Century**, July 1, 1953.

War II was the last war that all Americans fought with conviction. Thereafter, when "bombs bursting in air" would be atomic bombs, world war became a suicidal risk. Wars that could be so final and swift lost their glamour even for the most militaristically minded. When we became the most powerful nation on earth, the old insecurity that made patriotism into a condi- tioned reflex of "my country right or wrong" should have given way to a thinking process; as expressed by Carl Schurz: "Our country...when right, to be kept right. When wrong, to be put right." It was not until the Indochina war that we began the search for a new kind of patriotism.

If we are to find true and concrete meaning in patriotism, I suggest these starting points. **First**, in order that a free and just consensus be formed, patriotism must once again be rooted in the individual's own conscience and beliefs. Love is conceived by the giver (citizens) when merited by the receiver (the governmental authorities). If ''consent of the governed'' is to have any meaning, the abstract ideal of country has to be separated from those who direct it; otherwise the government cannot be evaluated by its citizens. The authorities in the State Department, the Pentagon, or the White House are not infallible; they have been and often are wrong, vain, misleading, shortsighted or authoritarian. When they are, leaders like these are shortchanging, not representing, America. To identify America with them is to abandon hope and settle for tragedy. Americans who consider themselves patriotic in the traditional sense do not usually hesitate to heap criticism in domestic matters over what they believe is oppressive or wasteful or unresponsive government handling of their rights and dignity. They should be just as vigilant in weighing similar government action which harnesses domestic resources for foreign involvements. Citizenship has an obligation to cleanse patriotism of the misdeeds done in its name abroad.

The flag, as the Pledge of Allegiance makes clear, takes its meaning from that ''for which it stands''; it should not and cannot stand for shame, injustice and tyranny. It must not be used as a bandanna or a fig leaf by those unworthy of this country's leadership.

Second, patriotism begins at home. Love of country in fact is inseparable from citizen action to make the country more lovable. This means working to end poverty, discrimination, corruption, greed and other conditions that weaken the promise and potential of America.

Third, if it is unpatriotic to tear down the flag (which is a symbol of the country), why isn't it more unpatriotic to desecrate the country itself — to pollute, despoil and ravage the air, land and water? Such environmental degradation makes the ''pursuit of happiness'' ragged

211

"IT WAS DESIGNED AS A FLAG, BUDDY — NOT AS A BLINDFOLD."

indeed. Why isn't it unpatriotic to engage in the colossal waste that characterizes so many defense contracts? Why isn't it unpatriotic to draw our country into a mistaken war and then keep extending the involvement, with untold casualities to soldiers and innocents, while not telling Americans the truth? Why isn't the deplorable treatment of returning veterans by government and industry evaluated by the same standards as is their dispatch to war? Why isn't the systematic contravention of the U.S. Constitution and the Declaration of Independence in our treatment of minority groups, the poor, the young, the old and other disadvantaged or helpless people crassly unpatriotic? Isn't all such behavior contradicting the innate worth and the dignity of the individual in America? Is it not time to end the tragic twisting or patriotism whereby those who work to expose and correct deep injustices, and who take intolerable risks while doing it, are accused of running down America by the very forces doing just that? Our country and its ideals are something for us to uphold as individuals and together, not something to drape, as a deceptive cloak, around activities that mar or destroy these ideals.

Fourth, there is no reason why patriotism has to be so heavily associated, in the minds of the young as well as adults, with military exploits, jets and missiles. Citizenship must include the duty to advance our ideals actively into practice for a better community, country and world, if peace is to prevail over war. And this obligation stems not just from a secular concern for humanity but from a belief in the brotherhood of man — "I am my brother's keeper" — that is common to all major religions. It is the classic confrontation — barbarism vs. the holy ones. If patriotism has no room for deliberation, for acknowledging an individual's sense of justice and his religious principles, it will continue to close minds, stifle the dissent that has made us strong, and deter the participation of Americans who challenge in order to correct, and who question in order to answer. We need only to recall recent history in other countries where patriotism was converted into an epidemic of collective madness and destruction. A patriotism manipulated by the government asks only for a servile nod from its subjects. A new patriotism requires a thinking assent from its citizens. If patriotism is to have any "manifest destiny," it is in building a world where all mankind is our bond in peace.

ABILITY TO EMPATHIZE

The ability to empathize, to see life and its problems through another person's eyes, is a skill you must develop if you intend to learn from the experiences of others.

Consider the following true life situation:

THE FLAG SALUTE *

Susan Russo, a high school teacher at Sperry High School in Henrietta, New York, was well qualified and impressed her principal when she was hired. As a teacher, just about everybody agreed, she did very well. She fared badly, nevertheless, because of "irreconcilable conceptions of patriotism." Each day in her school began with the pledge of allegiance to the flag recited over the school's public address system. During the ceremony Mrs. Russo stood silently with her hands at her side. She made no issue of her refusal to say the pledge and place her hand over her heart; she merely didn't do it.

> I didn't agree with the wording of the Pledge, and it was a matter of my own personal conscience, and I couldn't be hypocritical about what I believed in...I am generally proud to be an American, but I object to saying the Pledge for basically two reasons. First of all, I don't think that anyone can demand the recitation of an oath of allegiance. I think loyalty is better proved through daily actions and the way you behave as an

* David Sanford, "In Conscience," **The New Republic**, June 22, 1974, pp. 24-25.

American citizen, but more importantly, I object to the actual
wording of the Pledge, because the words "liberty and justice
for all" are inaccurate, and I feel we are hypocritical in saying
that as a truth.

Mrs. Russo was observed by her principal. When
confronted with his disapproval she wouldn't recon-
sider her refusal and was asked to resign. When she did
not, and since she was not tenured, she was
terminated.

> **I pledge allegiance to the flag of the United States
> of America and to the Republic for which it stands,
> one nation under God, indivisible, with liberty and
> justice for all.**

Instructions

Try to imagine how the following individuals would
react in this situation. What reasons would they give for
their actions? Try to imagine and explain their feelings.

Susan Russo

Principal

Group of students protesting the requirement that they
recite the pledge

Author of reading 23

Author of reading 24

School superintendent

Local teachers' association

You

Others

CHAPTER

WHAT AMERICA NEEDS

Readings

26. Developing Values In a Valueless Society
   Charles W. Anderson

27. What Is Right With America
   George S. Benson

28. American Values In a Revolutionary World
   Warren Bryan Martin

29. Who Will Speak for America
   Earl Butz

DEVELOPING VALUES IN A VALUELESS SOCIETY

Charles W. Anderson

Charles W. Anderson is the Coordinator, Alcohol-
ism and Drug Abuse Services, County of Rock,
Rock County Hospital and Rock Haven, Janesville,
Wisconsin. The following reading was delivered as
a speech at Commencement, George S. Parker
High School, Janesville, Wisconsin, June 6, 1972.

Use the following questions to assist your reading:

1. Why does the author believe that knowledge of self
   is important?
2. How has society made life more difficult by stifling
   emotions?
3. Why does the author feel love is the most important
   emotion in developing values?
4. How does the author suggest the individual develop
   a system of values in our value-less society?

Charles W. Anderson, ''Developing Values in a Value-less
Society,'' **Vital Speeches of the Day**, July 15, 1972, page 600-02.
Reprinted with permission.

Know Thyself

I would like to address myself to how you can develop a system of values in a valueless society.

I work in an alcoholic treatment center which is housed in a mental institution complex. Each day I see what society can do to those human beings who are less resilient than those of us who are usually but not necessarily correctly referred to as "normal" people. My interest in these less fortunate people was developed as the result of my own experiences of many years as a drinking alcoholic and my experiences also as the son of an active alcoholic who ultimately died from it.

There was a Jesuit philosopher who wrote wisely about the phenomenon of man and the future of man. Pierre Teilhard de Chardin argued that the evolutionary process on earth has stopped as far as man's physical development is concerned and that the earth's evolutionary capacity is concerned now with the growth of the human spirit. Teilhard maintained that man will continue to grow in spiritual capacity and one day he will become one with his fellow man and be then aware of God as never before. He believed that at the ultimate point, man would not lose his individuality but, rather, gain it. He would gain it through evaluation of his thoughts and their influence for good on other human beings.

This was not a new idea. Socrates urged his audience to "know thyself." Plato learned from him and taught the same. Plutarch and Solon advised similarly. Alfred Lord Tennyson said it too in a favorite poem of mine.

> Flower in the crannied wall,
> I pluck you out of the crannies.
> I hold you here, root and all, in my hand,
> Little flower — but if I could understand,
> What you are, root and all, and all in all,
> I should know what God and man is.

Obviously, wise men through the ages felt that knowledge of self was a prerequisite to understanding others. Unfortunately, we spend so little time doing that in our go-go world. And when we do, so infrequently, we measure ourselves against a societal model. I believe we need to develop a system of personal values against which to measure ourselves.

I'd like to share with you today, two things that are based on and are the product of my very personal experiences. First, I wish to share my feelings with you. Emotions are things we are taught to control or, better yet, to hide; we are told they are only for very private occasions — the intimacy of the family, or the bedroom; we are taught they should never be displayed in public. We are told there is something shameful and even unmanly about them. Men tend to excuse emotional displays in women as the result of some type of inferior mental mechanism or, illogically, to an inherent lack of logic in women. Many women, in reaction to this unjust and unwise attitude, attempt to stifle a quality that truly puts them above men in the ongoing process of human spiritual development.

Society tends to cripple our emotions each day. We are taught to hold back. Did you ever hear people laugh uncomfortably at an emotional scene in a movie? Think of how on television a scene can be developing, perhaps involving the very soul of a human being, and it is interrupted insensitively to have the virtues of a motor oil or panty hose extolled. Emotions are not allowed to be nurtured. If you are a boy and you cry, you are a sissy. If a girl cries, you are told to expect such nonsense from women.

We now can see young men killed in a "live" war while we have our dinner. We aren't given time to reflect on the passing of a life — a life that could have been filled with love and good. It is not a son, or a husband or a father or a brother who dies on our battlefields, it is a statistic and the message is that we got more of "them" than they did of "us." When is the last time any of us cried for a young man as he died in war? It is happening every day.

People with "crippled" or suppressed emotions tend to become neurotic, they often seek escape from tensions with drugs and alcohol. Some have the psychological and spiritual strength to survive this endless process and battle for some peace of mind in an insane world that allows little respite. However, our mental institutions and alcoholic treatment centers are filled with those who are not quite so strong. I hasten to add

219

> **How then can we develop a system of values that will serve us and society well; that will make us, as individuals, happy. One, beware of the corporate gods bearing gifts...Two, look for the truth about yourself; it is not easy to find but it's worth looking hard for. Three, fill your heart with emotions that are good for you. Then show them to others.**

this strength comes not from will power, personally developed, but from a combination of genetic factors and fortuitous environmental influences in the formative years. None of us can truly take for granted being outside these institutions. All of us are, ultimately, vulnerable.

I choose not to cripple my emotional life any more than it has already been by society. I tell you therefore how I feel. I am thrilled that you should ask me to speak at your commencement. I am hopeful that I can say something worthwhile. I've thought long and hard for I want to leave a lasting impression. I could cry when I think of the millions of young people who are turned off by what they face. Who truly believe there is no hope for a better world. This is why I so deeply desire that you will respond with a determination to be someone with values and someone of value in this value-less society of ours. There is a future for all of us, if we just open our hearts.

This brings me now to those thoughts I wish to share. Hopefully my thoughts will change from time to time — hopefully, also, they will always change for the better. Never, I hope, will my thoughts be based on anything other than my own values. These values I hope will always be reflected in my behavior and emotions. Emotions or thoughts without a system of values are value-less. We must seek therefore to develop a system of values.

Love Thyself

Love in my judgment is the most basic emotion yielding good to the individual and society, and it is the bedrock for all our other values. It is unfortunate that we have equated love with sex for love transcends sex. Men may love men, women may love women and not be homosexual. Man should love man. Christ urged us all to do unto others as we would have them do unto us. Man has made the mistake of thinking that obeying such an injunction will put him in the class of the martyr. Nothing could be farther from the truth. Think of those things which make you feel good. Do you feel best when you do something good for someone else or when you hurt someone? If you answer the latter, you had best beware for you haven't looked deeply enough. All evidence indicates good acts, acts of kindness, integrity, loyalty, produce good personal feelings about self. As we do good things we develop a love of self, not a selfish love of demanding and getting, but the love of self which comes from knowing you have done right. Feeling worthy is what William Glasser the proponent of reality therapy would call it.

It is from this love of self that love for others flows. Alcoholics have a suicide rate which is 58 times greater than the average. Their hate for themselves is of the deepest intensity. And they all feel alienated — unable to love others, though they yearn to so desperately. When they discover they are the victims of a disease and are not moral weaklings, the first opportunity for self love develops, and miracle of miracles, they learn they can love others too.

We cannot love others if we hate ourselves; we can hardly teach others to love if our own hearts are empty. How then do we develop love for self. I repeat, we do it through doing those things which make us feel good. I am not speaking of things we may say make us feel good after only superficial and shallow thought like buying a bigger house, a swimming pool, a new car. We must dig deep into our minds and hearts and know ourselves as we are. Shakespeare wrote:

> This above all: To thine own self be true,
> And it must follow as the night the day,
> Thou canst not then be false to any man.

True to self thus true to others; love for self, thus love for others, follows as the night the day.

I know some cynics will sneer and say we delude

ourselves. Love conquers all things we are told but they know it is not true. Love has not conquered all things. We know it too. But we can hope that love *will* conquer all things. Hate is a destructive force; it tears one apart against others and these actions may be successful at the moment. Hitler was successful and conquered many — his hate killed millions of humans. But it also destroyed him. I do not equate his ultimate demise with the deaths of millions as far as justice is concerned. They were innocent and justice was not theirs. But Hitler never found what he sought, which was happiness for himself. He became in fact a madman. And that unfortunately is where our world is headed. Mass paranoia, schizophrenia, depression, alcoholism and drug abuse are already here. Escapism is the order of the day. Each of us is alone and withdrawing more and more. But John Donne warned us:

> "No man is an island, entire of itself; every man is a piece of the continent, a part of the main" and also "any man's death diminishes me, because I am involved in mankind; and therefore never send to know for whom the bell tolls; it tolls for thee."

If the world is allowed to go to hell; it goes to hell for all of us.

Think For Yourself

Let me warn you not to depend on society to serve as your guide for developing values. Society cheats us every day. It urges us to get away from self rather than to seek self. Booze and pills will relieve your tension, take away your fear, help you sleep, help you with sex. Television and endless sports spectacles numb your mind. Forget, forget is the subliminal chant of entertainment entrepreneurs whose only interest is money, not you.

Society tells us to avoid truthfulness, if need be. Politicians take polls on issues and then tell you what you want to hear, not what they believe. President John Kennedy, a victim of our sick society, wrote a book called "Profiles in Courage." He extolled a handful of men for putting their integrity above political expediency. What a sad commentary that so few could be

SOCRATES, JESUS,
AND THE AMERICAN IDEAL

What are we worth as a people? Are we to be admired or despised? In my opinion, America has today no need so great as that of seeing her life in relation to her own ideal of life. What, then, is the American Ideal?...

It seems to me that the most striking feature of the modern mind, as against the ancient, is its loss of use of the term "Spirit." For the Greeks and the Jews who most powerfully influenced our forefathers, the separation of spirit and matter was primary and fundamental. For them the human world was two worlds. And their problem, both in thought and in action, was that of keeping these two realms in right relations one to another. To make the body of man the servant of his soul, to keep the outer world subservient to the inner life — that was the dominant aspiration of the cultures from which our own has sprung. But with the coming of the modern sciences, the modern industries, that dualism has by the loss of one of its members diminished to the very point of vanishing....

The sciences think in, and only in, external relations. The industries, following their scientific leaders, deal with human beings more and more in merely material terms. Together they have driven the words of the spirit out of our calculations....

Now the question here involved can be very simply stated. It is this: Did Socrates and Jesus, the Greek and the Jew, talk nonsense? Are the words of Ecclesiasticus, of Isaiah, of Buddha, of Francis of Assisi, of Roger Williams, of Thomas Jefferson, now meaningless? And on this point my own conviction is deep and passionate. I am convinced that to speak of America, in terms of its spirit, as against the terms of material welfare, is to use that form of speech which, among all our ways of speaking, is most significant. To see

American life in terms of aspiration and of disappointment, to measure it as admirable or contemptible, to think of it as meeting or failing to meet its obligations — that is the one really important approach to an understanding of the nation....

We ought, I think, to study such men as Socrates and Jesus. These two men had genius in the examination of the spiritual life. Each was a thinker of the highest order. Just as Galileo, Newton, Darwin, Loeb, excel in intellectual mastery of the world of outer fact, so do these two surpass their fellows in the search for human wisdom....

It is recorded of the great Greek and of the great Jew that they went about among their fellows, talking with them of the values which they had found in human experience, and then pondering, meditating upon what they had seen and heard....

Both of them sought acquaintance with men and their intentions. Both tried to weave this information into a scheme of meaning, to understand, to interpret human purposes in ways of which they found those purposes to be sorely in need.

Out of these two studies there came what are, I think, the two most fruitful insights which Western civilization has known. For men who are forever asking, "What shall I be and do?" Socrates summed up his wisdom in the phrase, "Be intelligent; act critically." And Jesus, likewise pondering on human action, said to his fellows, "Be kind." And in terms of sheer domination over the mind of the Western world no other pair of intellectual achievements can equal these two....

Out of them came the two great practical tests which we apply to any proposal of action, any social institution, any individual attitude. First we demand, with Socrates, "Is it intelligent or is it stupid?'' Second we ask with Jesus, ''Does it spring from hate and indifference, or does it come from love?''...

We need to understand America. We must try, therefore, to think in the terms of Socrates and Jesus. We need to interpret our national life in terms of the spirit. We must find and make clear, therefore, our ideals — the stuff of which the spirit is made.

Reprinted from **What Does America Mean?** by Alexander Meiklejohn. By permission of W. W. Norton & Company, Inc. Copyright 1935 by W. W. Norton & Company, Inc. Copyright renewed 1963 by Donald Meiklejohn.

found. The message of today is do not search for truth but for opinion. In a speech to the Electors of Bristol, in 1774, Edmund Burke said: ''Your representative owes you, not his industry only, but his judgment; and he betrays instead of serving you if he sacrifices it to your opinion.''

Business tells us to buy its endless parade of goods, and to think only of material things and the satisfaction of our wants not our needs. Poor quality and planned obsolescence is routine procedure. Profit is king. Business, especially through Madison Avenue, lies to us each day and pays our neighbors to do it. And students, beware, for it is prepared to pay you too! William Wordsworth said it long ago.

> The world is too much with us; late and soon,
> Getting and spending, we lay waste our powers;
> Little we see in Nature that is ours.

Our schools too frequently ignore reality and merely serve as reinforcers of the status quo. Five years ago Red China was our implacable enemy and for all practical purposes you couldn't learn about it in school. Now we have started overtures of friendship. Surely our schools will now start more intensive studies of Red China! Industry has lent itself to this effort with plans for getting this new market for its goods. Which thought came first — the need for friendship or the need for markets? One can wonder.

Even our churches have failed in many cases. It is only recently they have started to seek Christian answers to social problems. Dishonesty, greed, hate, hypocrisy run rampant.

How then can we develop a system of values that will serve us and society well; that will truly make us, as individuals, happy? **One**, beware of the corporate gods bearing gifts — comfort is pleasant but luxury is decadent. We do not need an endless array of electric toothbrushes, electric blankets, electric mixers, electric fans, electric thises and electric thats, washers and dryers, and three, not two cars, and television sets for every person in the family. I suggest we have been oversold on relieving ourselves of physical chores. We are urged to join health clubs and country clubs to get exercise and then we use motor driven cycles or electric golf carts to take the physical effort out of exercise. Paradox after paradox fills our lives.

Two, look for the truth about yourself; it is not easy to find but it's worth looking hard for. **Three**, fill your heart with emotions that are good for you. Then show them to others. Do not be ashamed of them. Tell your fellow man — I love you. Feel worthwhile about yourself, love yourself and then love others.

Remember if we want to make a better world, we must first make better selves. If we ourselves are filled with greed and hate, how can we teach generosity and love?

Let us all change only ourselves. That is not an insurmountable task. If each of us would change ourselves, the whole world would be changed. But even if only we change, we at least are the victors. Develop your values for yourself and the world will be better for it.

Integrity in business and politics can become the rule rather than the exception. Men and women can look at each other with trust rather than suspicion. Your children can look to the future as a challenge rather than an impending doom.

Fill your hearts with the wonder of life and the joys it can bring. Don't let anyone tell you it can't be done, tell them it will be done.

WHAT IS RIGHT WITH AMERICA

George S. Benson

> George S. Benson is an educator who served as a missionary to China for many years. He was also the president of Harding College from 1936 until 1965. He now produces a weekly radio program, **Behind the News**. He has received several awards from Freedoms Foundation and is an authority on Oriental religions and philosophy. His articles appear in many religious and secular publications.

Consider the following questions while reading:

1. Why does the author believe that America has been successful in providing freedom and economic well-being?
2. Why is the author proud of our spiritual heritage?
3. What role must religion play in America, in the author's opinion?
4. What does the author see as the challenge to America? Do you agree with his analysis?

George S. Benson, ''What Is Right With America,'' an undated pamphlet distributed by The National Education Program.

The Priceless Values

Our fathers in the Declaration of Independence recognized that liberty is from God and that it is an innate gift, a gift which man has no right to destroy. The constitution undertook to preserve this liberty. Now we have enjoyed it for six generations and consequently, we tend to forget its value — just as almost anything that man long possesses he ceases to properly treasure.

But when we think soberly we ourselves recognize that freedom is exceedingly important. It is one of the big things. Therein lies the very foundation for our happiness and our prosperity.

Man's next big desire is for economic well-being. All men want adequate food, clothing, housing, entertainment, transportation, automobiles, radios, telephones, refrigerators — yes, we all want economic well-being. At this point, three facts are very, very important to recognize:

1. Production is the only source of wealth.

2. High productivity is the key to increasing wealth.

3. A competitive private enterprise economy is the key to high productivity.

Private Ownership

Our private enterprise economy allows any man to start producing any useful product at his will, and allows for him a free market in which he can dispose of his product. We also have the freedom to compete with every dreamer. When Henry Ford started producing low cost automobiles and they began to sell in great numbers, many other people also entered the field to produce low-cost automobiles. In fact, hundreds of companies were formed to manufacture automobiles during the past 80 years....

Highest Living Standard

Our high productivity gives us a high standard of living that is proverbial. For instance, our national income equals that of the next highest six countries combined. Our average per capita income is now $3,600. About one-half of the people of the world are living on a per capita income of less than $100 a year. The people of Western Europe live on an income of about $1,5000 to $1,800 a year. Russians live on a per capita income of about $800 a year.

While America has only 6% of the world's population she graduates from high school as many as all the rest of the world combined. Likewise, America graduates from college more young people than does the other 94% of the world combined. This is because it is only in America that the head of a family can earn enough money to send his children to high school and to college, while he supplies food, housing, clothing, medical care, and entertainment for the family. It is only in America that a man working on hourly wages can hope to earn the money to pay for a home, an automobile, a radio, a telephone, a refrigerator, and to send his son and daughter to college.

So, if it is personal freedom and economic well-being that we want most, then we should by all means preserve the American system which has provided them in degrees never before experienced by any segment of the human race.

Our Spiritual Heritage

It is not enough however to have personal freedom and economic well-being. The ox in the stall may be very happy if well fed and watered and sheltered. Man however is not content just to be free and economically well-off. Man also desires spiritual values, which in like manner are best satisfied in America. For instance, we have great religious freedom which is real — not just theoretical. The Bible remains the best seller among all books in America. It reveals man's origin, his function in this life, and his final destiny. Approximately 60% of all American people have their names on church rolls and approximately 40% are accustomed to going to church.

Fruits of our spiritual heritage include most of the hospitals, which are privately supported; homes for widows and orphans, most of which are privately supported; unparalleled concern for the poor which is now quite largely government supported, but by taxes voted by the people and their representatives. Some thirteen billion dollars is being spent for direct relief; gnawing hunger is unnecessary in any part of our country. While it is sometimes stated that 15% of our people are below the poverty line, it means that 85% then are not poor; and the poor are receiving the most liberal aid that the poor ever received anywhere in the world.

Benefactor of Mankind

These are the three main values — personal freedom, economic well-being, a rich spiritual heritage — and America provides all three of them to the greatest degree ever known in the history of mankind. Western Europe is approximately 50% socialized and has an average income about half of our own. Russia is thoroughly and completely socialized and has a per capita income approximately a fourth of our own.

While Communism is a great enemy of capitalism, yet it is certainly a very poor second in providing the things that man wants most.

The criticism leveled at America by either her enemies or her friends should be given very careful consideration. We should work to improve America in every way we can, but we are not justified in joining our enemies in the attempt to destroy America.

It is sometimes argued that we do not have a good distribution of wealth and of course, it is true that we do not have a perfect distribution of wealth. No nation does have or ever has had or ever will have perfect distribution of wealth. But we have the best distribution in America to be found in any country. We have a very small and diminishing class of rich people and we have a small and diminishing class of truly poor. We have a great growing middle class with the greatest prosperity that any middle class ever experienced. We should not be content, however. We should keep working for a better distribution of the good things of life but we shouldn't destroy the system that has produced the best that man has yet known. We should work to improve it in any way we can.

A few decades ago the socialists made a great point of "The greatest good for the greatest number." They

TRADITIONAL VALUES

Traditionally, American culture with its strong fibres of freedom and progress has been nourished by religious ideals; our heritage is a love of liberty and a faith in God. Over many years Americans generally maintained a wholesome attitude toward religious values. But today, as never before in our history, these values that made our Country great are being challenged. There is in this land another so-called "value" emerging. It is the idea that nothing is right or wrong; it all depends on the situation. This kind of thinking has caused disruption on our campuses and rioting in our streets.

Mrs. Frank Roger Seaver, "Traditional Values That Live!" an undated pamphlet distributed by Americanism Educational League.

have quit arguing that in America because our capitalist system is the one that has obtained the greatest good for the greatest number. As a result I have heard no socialist quote that statement in a long time.

Not Perfect

It may well be argued that our American system does not work perfectly, and it is true that there are inequalities and that there are unpunished crimes, etc. At this point we should remember, however, that there is no perfect political, economic, religious, or social system. This is because of the imperfections of man. We will always have some people who hypocritically take advantage of the possibilities under any system.

Because of the imperfections of man, perfection will not be achieved in this world. Capitalism has its weaknesses but Communism has far more. Therefore, as Americans we should support the system that has worked for us so well and which has enabled us to achieve, as no other people have ever achieved, the basic values in life.

Marriage was ordained of God. The family unit is the most essential unit in all civilized society, but marriage doesn't work perfectly. On the contrary, about one in four marriages in America goes on the rocks. Perhaps another 25% are not totally happy. Nevertheless, we should continue to encourage marriage. We should not decide to throw overboard the system and turn to free love which would be far worse. Likewise the church, ordained of God, is not functioning perfectly because of the imperfections of man. Who knows of a single congregation where the leaders are all perfect and the membership is all perfect and everything works perfectly. None of us do. Shall we therefore, throw overboard religion because it doesn't work perfectly — not by any means. On the contrary, religion offers our one best hope. It is essential to building the kind of character that makes it possible to enjoy the blessings we now have in America and it offers the one hope to have a better America.

The Challenge

I appeal to each of you:

1. Do everything you know how to do to be a good citizen and to help make America a still better place to live.

2. Don't join the revolutionaries to help tear down the best system that man has yet developed.

The stakes are very high. If we can keep our own people sold on our own American way of life and defeat the revolutionaries and achieve reasonable harmony and understanding between the major segments of our own society, then our productivity can go up 100% in the next 25 years, thus doubling our current standard of living. We can expand our spiritual heritage, overcome the growing crime wave, alcoholism, misuse of drugs, etc. and achieve to a still greater measure the good things that our Creator has made possible for us; and there would be no World War III.

If on the contrary, we remain hypnotized in lethargy and the Communists win their objectives, then it will be a godless world, a totalitarian world and the dark ages all over again.

What is right with America? The great fundamental principles are right. The mechanism of our Republic is right. The privately owned economic system is right. The message of God as expressed in the Bible is right.

Let us improve the human element, support our Godgiven freedom, and work for a peaceful and prosperous world.

AMERICAN VALUES IN A REVOLUTIONARY WORLD

Warren Bryan Martin

This reading was originally delivered as a speech at the Northern Region Conference of the California Scholarship Federation in 1965. At the time Mr. Martin was provost of Raymond College, University of the Pacific.

The following questions will help you examine the reading:

1. Why does the author feel that optimism, a traditional American trait, is disappearing?
2. Why does the author feel success is not a satisfying value?
3. Why is the American attachment to security a hazard in today's revolutionary world?
4. What role does the church play in modern America, in the author's opinion?
5. What qualities does the author feel are important to those who would build a proper life philosophy?

Warren Bryan Martin, "American Values In A Revolutionary World," **Vital Speeches of the Day**, July 15, 1965, page 588-92. Reprinted with permission.

The Decline of Optimism

I propose to comment today on what is happening to traditional American values in an epoch of revolutionary change....

An incisive analysis of American values in a revolutionary world will cost you $10.80. That is the price of Saul Bellow's novel, **Herzog**, and Norman Mailer's novel, **An American Dream**. I am not being flippant. An epoch reveals itself most lucidly in its art forms and that which comes to us via these media is a revelation of man in his times. These two recent novels tell us a great deal about what it means to be an American in...the Twentieth Century.

The central character in each book — Moses Herzog in one, and Steven Rojack in the other — is a man disillusioned with American values and desperate for a new life. They live in a time when it seems that the bottom has dropped out of the barrel. But let me try to be more specific about the form and extent of their disillusionment.

The traditional American philosophy of life, as Robert Heilbruner and others have emphasized, has been a philosophy of optimism, grounded in the faith that the historic environment was congenial or at least neutral to man's efforts. Thus, man's efforts could mold the future. Man was not "fated," but "free."...

But now all of that is changing. The philosophy of optimism is being sorely challenged even in this country. While Americans have said that man is "free," now we feel more and more "fated." We cannot unilaterally control the new technology of war, for example. Vast social forces are reshaping the world and we seem unable to control them. We have believed that we could mold history — but history is not conforming to our will in China, or even in Cuba. We have had the certainty that moral alternatives are obvious to men of good will, not ambiguous, but today we have great trouble finding a course of action that is morally consistent, let alone one toward which we can have the certainty of the right. We are confused....

Success

If Americans have been traditionally oriented to

optimism, they have also traditionally placed success high in their hierarchy of values.

At first glance it may appear that Americans are more oriented to the pleasure-principle than to anything else. It is true that modern man has put his faith in the pleasure-principle. This is natural. We are all born with built-in pleasure-pain reactors. We ignore them to our hurt. We know that the body and the world hold immense possibilities for enjoyment.

But the truth of the matter is that our society is not willing to accept pleasure on its own terms. The evidence that we are more oriented to success than the pleasure-principle is the fact that we want our pleasures carefully controlled. It is more important for us to succeed in them than to submit to them. Enjoyment is contingent on success.

And on what terms? Our traditional values have emphasized that success should be in terms of wealth, fame, or power. Now success in terms of wealth, fame, and power is not to be scorned or condemned. Success is a social achievement, tied in with the lives of others. But what the novelists show us in the two books to which I am today referring is that wealth, fame, power are exclusive. They inevitably create division. Furthermore, they are always competitive. And because they are competitive, they are precarious satisfactions. They come, they go. Here is the paradox: with these values you always want more. "Success is a goal without a satiation point," says the psychologist Abram Kardiner. Yet on the other hand, the more you seek these "satisfactions" the more they lose their ability to satisfy. Success is, like pleasure, fleeting and fading. Both novels — **Herzog** and **An American Dream** — chronicle the extent to which our society has been in the grip of a success syndrome.

Security

Another value tied in with our traditional interest in success is our concern for security. Man has always been more concerned for security than liberty. Throughout history if a choice must be made between security and freedom, the majority of men choose security. Now the uncertainty of our age — the fact that we live in a world where our way of life is threatened by

236

"THINGS"
AND THE GOOD LIFE

The things most prized and honored in America are the expanding production of wealth, whether or not the wealth produced satisfies real needs or artificially induced wants; technological advances either for their own sake or for the sake of creature comforts and conveniences in excess of genuine need; external or worldly success as measured by the acquisition of money, fame, or power rather than development of the inner man and the growth of the human being as a person; the expansion of the sensate life rather than the intensification of the life of the mind. The high value set upon these things represents a fundamental disorder of goods, a perverse scale of values, placing lower over higher goods, mistaking merely apparent for real goods, and even transforming goods that are only means into ends to be sought for their own sake, as if they constituted the good life as a whole.

Mortimer Adler, **The Time of Our Lives** (New York: Holt, Rinehart & Winston, 1970), pp. 223-24.

a war-god who can spit nuclear mucous on everybody; in a world of political ferment where we are confronted by the challenge of rival ideologies; in a world of revolutionary moral and ethical changes where we are faced with a value upheaval that results in ambiguity and paradox — the uncertainty of our times has heightened man's quest for security until we seem to be in the grip of a security-psychosis.

One consequence is a reaction to risk. So, we tend to shun mystery, we resent the new and unexpected except in the realm of things. We want human situations to be controlled even if it means the sacrifice of spontaneity, innovation and freedom. We are uneasy in the presence of novelty, although novelty is essential to the health of the human organism. We prefer to have our pleasures controlled — in a Disneyland where the steamboat runs on a track, and the train robbery is carefully staged; in dinner parties where the steak may be chateaubriand but where the conversation is more like cotton candy....

Power

Another traditional American value that is challenged today is our addiction to power. At the level of the individual, we have believed that if man will spit on his hands and flex his muscles he can prevail against formidable odds. At the level of our collective life, we have increasingly taken the position that power persuades, particularly technological and nuclear power. In Viet Nam it appears that the best answer we seem able to make to Communist ingenuity is the imposition of American power....

Confidence In Man and the Church

Underlying traditional American values has been a confidence in man, his capabilities, his essential worth, his intrinsic religious faith based on belief in God and belief in man. But now we have lost that confidence in man, even as we have lost contact with God. Religion once gave meaning to man, but we live in a secular age, one in which the traditional supports of religion have given way, and man stands alone, just at that moment in his history when he has least confidence in his ability to stand alone....

We may look to the art forms to document the extent to which a coherent image of man has been lost in modern times. In art, in abstract expressionism, for example, we have no coherent image of man. The traditional image of man is flayed, cut up in bits, strewn around like Osiris in ancient Egyptian mythology. But in modern art the image of man does not coalesce or come together in any recognizable way. If you go back to the ancient Greeks you can see in their statuary the confidence that they had in the dignity of man and the beauty of the human form. The medieval art forms also reflect the image of man in that time. They show the confidence that this God-intoxicated and Church-oriented age had that the human could be transfigured by the divine. In the Renaissance period we see a revival of the old Hellenistic confidence in the human

238

form and the dignity and power of the human mind. But today, in abstract expressionism, there is no coherent image of man. I do not speak in criticism of this fact. I mean, rather, to emphasize that the art forms of today are trying to say to us that man is too complicated to be typed or to be encapsulated in any system or conceptualized framework.

> The reason for the Church's success with the middle class has not been that the Church has succeeded in transforming the middle class according to Christian values but that the middle class has succeeded in imposing its values on the Church and has thus made the Church over in its image. The consequence is irrelevant religiosity.

And in this hour of need, the Church has not been of much help. The Church has been in retreat since the Thirteenth Century, which was the Golden Age for Christendom. From that time to the present the Church has suffered a series of attacks that have drained its authority and self-confidence. If the Sixteenth Century saw the unitary Christian Church shattered by the Protestant Revolution, the Seventeenth and Eighteenth Centuries saw assaults on the Bible as the basis of religious authority and on Jesus Christ as the savior and example for all of mankind. In the Nineteenth Century came the attack on the existence of a personal God. Also, in the Nineteenth Century, the working man walked out of the Churches in great numbers throughout Western Europe because he saw that the Church was identified with the ruling hierarchy and the working man was in no mood to share communion with that group in society that denied to him basic human dignity and brotherhood. Again, the American experience has been somewhat different. The Church not only survived here but seemed to grow in strength and influence, particularly with the middle class. But the crest seems to have been passed in 1958 and the Church now appears to be declining in influence. But, more important, the reason for the Church's success with the middle class has not been that the Church has succeeded in transforming the middle class according to Christian values but that the middle class has succeeded in imposing its values on the Church and has thus made the Church over in its image. The consequence is irrelevant religiosity....

Well, all of this has been said in an effort to emphasize that modern man stands naked, as it were, stripped of his traditional consolations, and the mood of disillusionment, anxiety, and alienation...indicates that we don't like what we see of ourselves....

How To Build A Life Philosophy

Are you among those desperate for a new life? And are you willing to quest after it? If so, allow me to suggest what you should incorporate into your philosophy of life if you are to speak relevantly to an epoch of crisis.

First, you must be aware of the inevitability of value judgments. To be educated, for example, is not just to know something. It is to know something *important*. But when you qualify the noun knowledge with the adjective *important*, you have passed beyond fact to value. David Hume emphasized that we cannot pass from an ''is'' to an ''ought'' by logic. Because millions in the world are hungry, it does not follow that I ought to feed them. Whether I feed them or not will be determined by my hierarchy of values — values based on faith and fact. Thus, it is a false use of language to say that one is devoid of faith, that one need not make value judgments. Nonsense. To live is to confront options and make choices.

Right here we have a matter of special importance for young people. Edgar Friedenburg, a social scientist at Brooklyn College, says that today's students are not lazier or duller than earlier generations, but he does claim that they are less disciplined. And it is an inner discipline that is lacking. They have nothing at the core of their being by which to judge and discipline their lives. He blames society for this condition. Adolescence — that period in life when self-definition should take place, in which self-identity should be achieved — has almost vanished in this country because the young person is surrounded by a culture which gives him no sharp contrasts, no hierarchy of values, no set of options, by which to clarify his own experience, no sharp images against which to clarify his own experience, no sharp images against which to measure his own identity. In the American community instead of sharpening and clarifying, we blur and round off; when a conflict arises, we do not try to spell it out but rather rush in to mediate and especially to moderate it.

Now we must change that situation. We must face the fact that to live is to make value judgments. In a world characterized by ambiguity, we must nevertheless affirm and deny. We either do it consciously or life forces choices upon us.

A second point must be made. Those who are desperate for a new life that is relevant and responsible must accept the provisional nature of all value judgments.

While those who say they have no faith must be made to see the extent to which they have faith, it is also necessary to emphasize that faith is faith — not certainty. At the human level we have no absolute certainty about man and his values. At best we have only provisional certitudes. Please understand that this does not mean that we can be free from value commitments, our commitments are real and obligating, but it does mean that we must understand their provisional nature. It does mean that we must always be open to change — though not empty. It means that we will have commitments, but, given the ambiguity of reality and given the provisional nature of all value commitments due to the finitude of man, we will avoid what Galesworthy once called "cockeyed-cocksuredness" — that is the stance of the man who is sometimes wrong but never in doubt. Such arrogance is unpardonable....

What is the consequence of this style of life? Well, for one thing the challenge today is to live, to state it still another way, the life of *creative insecurity*. A commitment to creativity is a commitment to insecurity. But believing that there is no value more significant than creativity itself — that is, the freedom to use one's abilities to help bring into being what one believes to be good — then the risk of insecurity is taken.

241

It is true that we do not know much about fostering creativity, but we do know something about the traits shared by original people. *Openness* is one. The creative person says "yes" to life — to the exterior world and to the interior man. *Flexibility* is another trait of original people. They have a tolerance for ambiguity. *Independence* is still another quality. Creative people know that the man who leads must be willing to go it alone. *Courage* too, is a characteristic. Creative persons have courage, especially the courage to fail. They know that implicit in everything worth doing is the possibility of failure. Creative people also have what Richard Hofsteadter has called "an attitude of playfulness and piety" toward ideas. They try on new ideas, wear them about for fit, put them off, and try on something else. They move in the realm of ideas with a certain spontaneity and vivacity. Yet, they move in the world of ideas with respect bordering on piety.

There is another characteristic needed in the value system of the man who is questing for a new life. He must have human sensitivity. This is the ability to feel things deeply. It is sensitivity that can assure that creativity is used to dignify human life and not to destroy it....

Therein lies the tragedy of our times. We have lost the ability to love because we have lost confidence in our ability to have fruitful relationships with other human beings. How much has been lost when we lack the sensitivity to see through another's eyes and feel through another's heart....

Finally, the new man in the new age must be willing to incorporate the concept of changes in his philosophy of life. We live in a world or revolutionary upheaval, we find ourselves in a setting of ambiguity and uncertainty, therefore, the society equal to the challenges of this century will be the society in which continuous innovation can occur. We must learn to be unafraid of change. Indeed we must learn to embrace change as a positive value. For a summary statement, I have taken a quotation from the most recent book of Dr. John Gardner of the Carnegie Corporation of New York — the book is entitled **Self Renewal** — and the quotation reads as follows:

What good, what lasting good is there in me? Is there nothing else between birth and death but what I can get out of this perversity — only a favorable balance of disorderly emotions? No freedom? Only impulses? And what about all the good I have in my heart — doesn't it mean anything? Is it simply a joke? A false hope that makes a man feel the illusion of worth? And so he goes on with his struggles. But this good is no phony. I know it isn't. I swear it.

This is the challenge if we are to meet the needs of our society in a setting of revolutionary change.

WHO WILL SPEAK FOR AMERICA?

Earl L. Butz

Earl L. Butz has served as the U.S. Secretary of Agriculture since December, 1971. He is a former educator in agricultural economics at Purdue University and has authored numerous pamphlets, research bulletins and articles in magazines and journals. The following reading was originally delivered as a speech before the Polish Legion Veteran's Convention in 1974.

Bring the following questions to your reading:

1. Secretary Butz claims the American system works well. What evidence does he present to support his claim? Do you agree with his reasoning?
2. How do you think the author of the previous reading would react to the Secretary's remarks?
3. Why does the author feel America is a "good nation." Do you agree?

Earl L. Butz, "Who Will Speak for America," **Vital Speeches of the Day**, September 15, 1974, page 710-12. Reprinted with permission.

We are in this country because we believe it has something special to offer. That something special is freedom: the right of every man, woman, and child to live in peace and individual dignity, the right of every human being to pursue a livelihood and lifestyle of his or her own choice.

This is our system. It is a system that works.

Some have said that we are a violent people. *But who has done more to support the cause of peace in the world during the past five years?* Our President has gone to China, opening the doors of communication with 800 million people that were a mystery to most of the Western world. We are still ideologically on opposite sides of the fence with the People's Republic of China, but now we are talking and trading instead of fighting.

We have gained a detente with the world's second most powerful nation, the Soviet Union. Again, we are talking and trading instead of threatening. That interplay has helped reduce world tensions to the point where a negotiated peace is becoming a reality in the Middle East. Instead of World War III coming from last year's Arab-Israeli conflict — we have brought the two sides to the negotiating table. We could not have done that without some cooperation with the Soviet Union.

There are still dangerous tensions in the world, but because of America's sincere desire for peace the world is closer to global stability than it has been for many years.

Our agriculture is playing an important part in building that peace. Food is a language that leaps oceans and crosses borders; it pierces all barriers. It is the product that enables America to speak more forcefully, more powerfully, and more compassionately than any other nation in the world. I'm proud to play a small part in that agriculture.

We hear that our unemployment is rising, that people are out of work. *But whoever talks about the fact that 98 percent of all married heads of households now have jobs, or that only slightly over 5 percent of all Viet Nam veterans 20 to 34 years old remain unemployed.*

Think of that. Six years ago over 500,000 young American men were fighting in Southeast Asia. Today they are all home and all but a few have been reabsorbed into the work force with very little fuss or bother.

We also tend to ignore the strain our large population growth of the last 25 years has put on the job market.

In 1950 about 58 million people out of a total work force of 62.6 million had jobs. The average wage for non-supervisory workers was around $1.33 an hour, or about $53 a week.

By June of 1974, the work force had swollen to over 92 million. But in spite of that growth, a full 87 million were employed. The average non-supervisory workman's pay had risen to $4.17 an hour, or $154 a week. Our free enterprise economic system had kept up with the large growth of laborers seeking work, a fact we often forget.

Anyone who doesn't believe that there are job opportunities for people willing to work in this country should visit a developing country. He should talk to a man whose family must be supported by the amount of money the father can earn swinging a pick or a shovel, or from a small plot of land where he can afford no fertilizer or pesticides. Then he should also remember that there are no food stamps, no unemployment insurance, nor workman's compensation for that family.

We hear that our food costs too much, that it is of poor nutritional quality. *Whoever mentions that groceries take less of our paycheck today than they did twenty years ago?* Last year the average per capita, after-tax income was $4,195. Only 15.7 percent of that went for food. In 1953 the average per capita after-tax income was $1,583 and a full 22 percent of that had to go for groceries....

Another change we hear frequently is that our high-paced style of living and our use of technology and chemicals is killing us and making us prone to all sorts of horrid diseases. *What spokesman points out to those who would have us return to the "good old days" that our lifespans are increasing and that most of the terrible diseases that have plagued mankind for centuries no longer threaten us?*

What about the Black Death, the Red Death, the plagues that wiped our Medieval Europe and killed hundreds of thousands? There were no antibiotics, no rules of sanitation, no vaccines — just the "good old days" with no known preventatives or cures.

WHY WE HONOR AMERICA

There are many reasons why we honor America today.

First, we honor America because she has opened her heart and her doors to the distressed and the persecuted of the world....

Secondly, we honor America because she has been the most generous nation in history. We have shared our wealth and our faith with a world in need....

Thirdly, we honor America because she has never hidden her problems and faults. With our freedom of the press and open communications system, we don't sweep our sins under the rug....

Fourthly, we honor America because she is honestly recognizing and is courageously trying to solve her social problems....

Fifthly, we honor America because she defends the right of her citizens to dissent. Dissent is impossible in many countries of the world, whereas constructive dissent is the hallmark of our freedom in America....

Sixthly, we honor America because there is woven into the warp and woof of our nation faith in God.

Billy Graham, "The Unfinished Dream" **Christianity Today**, July 31, 1970, p. 20-21. Copyright 1970 by **Christianity Today**; reprinted by permission.

Think back to your own childhood, or the childhood of only 15 or 20 years ago. Remember whooping cough, diphtheria, the measles, the mumps? What about polio — remember that one? Or how about the farm worker who cut himself on a threshing machine or mower and died of tetanus? How about the poor soul who contracted some sort of lingering infection that put him through months of misery before finally finishing him — today, common antibiotics could have cleaned up that infection within a week.

In 1900 the life expectancy at birth in the country was 47.3 years. Today the life expectancy at birth is 71.0 years. If you make it to the ripe old age of 47, statistics say you can expect about another 30 years. That doesn't sound like our lifestyle is hurting us too much....

Measure our wealth in material comforts if you like. Ninety-six percent of our households have TV sets; 43 percent have color sets. Eighty percent of all households own cars; 30 percent have two or more. Seventy-two percent own washing machines. Eighty-four percent own refrigerators; almost all the rest live in rental units where such amenities are provided for them.

In April of this year, 20 percent of all households expected to buy a new car within a year. Twenty-six percent expected to buy a major appliance. Ten percent expected to buy a new house within 2 years.

Look at another front. We have heard a great deal of criticism about our educational system during the last few years. *Whoever talks about the continuing effort we make as a nation to assure that education is available to anyone who wants it?*

Providing a broad range or educational opportunities lies at the very heart of our beliefs. It lies at the very core of our goal to assure a livelihood and human dignity for all people. Each year we spend about 8 percent of our gross national product on education. We have 400,000 youngsters in nursery school, 2½ million in kindergarten, 28 million in elementary school, 14 million in high school, and 8 million in college. No other country has ever attempted quality education on that sort of a scale.

There are special programs for the visually and aurally handicapped, the speech impaired, the emotionally and socially maladjusted, the retarded, the gifted. All together about 3 million children are enrolled in special education classes.

There are continuing education classes, job-sponsored educational programs, professional seminars, night schools, week-end schools. The choice is limitless and available to all ages in all walks of life. If you want to improve yourself, all you' have to do to initiate the step is dial the phone or send a postcard. For the college student, many universities are now so flexible that he can just about write his own schedule, picking and choosing as he may.

I've spent much of my life in education. I believe in it; it's better than ever and it will continue to improve. To complain about lack of meaningful educational opportunities in the United States today is sheer folly. We have opportunity for improvement and social mobility in this country such as the world has never seen.

We're not in the perfect society; there is no such Utopia. There never has been; there never will be. There are still injustices, but let's stop this business of pointing a finger at ourselves and accusing ourselves all the time. Let's look at the progress we are making.

Look at the gains in civil rights during the last decade. Our minority groups are not yet where they should be, but they are far better off in terms of things they have, in employment opportunities and in the chance for social advancement than they were 10 years ago. We are on the move in the right direction.

Let's not forget our relationship with the rest of the worlds. *Who points out that America has always been ready to help people in trouble, wherever they may live, whatever their beliefs may be?*

When the flood comes, or the earthquake, or the famine; we are there to help with as much aid as we can give, as quickly as possible. During the past 20 years, the United States has contributed about $25 billion in food aid to the rest of the world.

People say, ''You did that just to get rid of your surpluses.'' But the real test came last year when we didn't have any surpluses. Did we continue our food aid programs? Yes, even when we had to go into the market and buy the commodities — we contributed almost $1 billion in food aid last year. Again this year there are no surpluses. But there is $1 billion in our agricultural budget for food relief. The United States continues to be a nation with a heart.

We are a good nation. We are a NATION UNDER GOD. That stands forth in all our dreams and goals.

> **Some have said that we are a violent people. But who has done more to support the cause of peace in the world during the past five years?**

But because of the turmoil of Watergate; the injustices, the dishonesty that has taken place on both sides of the political fence, the faith of many of our people and especially our younger people has been shaken.

I think we are finally coming out of all that. People are once again realizing that the great share of the members of this Administration in Washington are dedicated, honest people serving their country and humanity. The great share of the civil servants are that. The great share of the members of Congress are that. The great share of the state legislators, of county commissioners, of city councilmen are honest, God-fearing, capable, dedicated Americans.

That has always been true. The basic tissue of America is strong. The fundamental precepts from which this nation grew have not been washed away. Of all the nations of the world, we are indeed a NATION UNDER GOD. We are a nation of destiny.

As we approach our Bicentennial, we hark back to the idealism and the dreams of the Founding Fathers who were willing to sacrifice everything they had to achieve their dream. They signed the Declaration of Independence, that noble document which stated, *"in support of this Declaration, with a firm reliance on the protection of Divine Providence, we mutually pledge to each other our lives, our fortunes and our sacred honor.''*

To sign that was no idle gesture. To sign that was to put your life on the line. But those men believed in this new nation they were creating so completely that they were willing to put their lives on the line for it — and some of them ended up giving those lives. Let's not forget that.

The vast majority of Americans still believe in that dream. They are willing to sacrifice to protect it, to strengthen it, to perpetuate it....

Let's all speak out for America once again. Let's not be ashamed of our dreams or our accomplishments.

We're a great nation and there is work to be done.

UNDERSTANDING STEREOTYPES

Instructions

STEP 1. If you think any groups you are familiar with fit the descriptions below, put their names in the blanks. Add any groups and descriptions that are frequently used by people you know.

1. _____ are good students

2. _____ are emotional

3. _____ have rhythm

4. _____ all look alike

5. _____ are aggressive and pushy

6. _____ are shrewd business people

7. _____ are lazy

8. _____ are hot-tempered

9. _____

10. _____

11. _____

12. _____

STEP 2. A **stereotype** is an oversimplified or exaggerated description. It can apply to things or people and be favorable or unfavorable. Quite often stereotyped beliefs about racial, religious, and national groups are insulting and oversimplified. They are usually based on misinformation or lack of information. Discuss the following questions about step 1, and stereotyping in general.

1. What stereotypes did different class members use in the statements above?
2. Were the stereotypes based on reason or emotion?
3. What kind of situations tend to stereotype people?
4. Why does stereotyping exist?
5. Is stereotyping a positive or negative action?

APPENDIX A

SELECTED PERIODICAL BIBLIOGRAPHY

Because most school libraries have a rather limited selection of books on American values, the editor has compiled a bibliography of helpful and recent periodical articles. Most school libraries have back issues of periodicals for at least a few years, and it is hoped that the following entries will be of some help to the student who wants to study American values in more depth.

VALUES AND THE AMERICAN CONDITION

ATLAS	*The U.S. At 200,* **Atlas,** July 1975, p. 28.
Susan Busch	*Too Many Idealists Are Hypocrites!* **Seventeen,** February 1971, p. 40.
Center Magazine	The American Character, July/August 1974, p. 54.
Philip M. Crane	*The American Condition: Social Perspectives,''* **Vital Speeches,** January 15, 1973, p. 194.
Porter Crow	*Finding Our Moral Compass,* **Vital Speeches,** August 15, 1974, p. 670.
John Z. Delorean	*Fulfilling the Reality of America,* **Vital Speeches,** February 1, 1972.
Hedley Donovan	*Who Is America? What Are We All About?* ' **Fortune,** April 1969, p. 83.
Harold P. Ford	*The Sleazing of America,* **Christian Century,** August 21, 1974, p. 796.
Norman C. Gaddis	*Our Survival As A Nation: Our Moral and Spiritual Values,* **Vital Speeches,** May 15, 1974, p. 479.
Billy Graham	*The Unfinished Dream,* **Christianity Today,** July 31, 1970, p. 31.

Ed. W. Hiles	*What's Happening To The Spirit of America?* ' **Vital Speeches**, March 15, 1972, p. 333.
Eric Hoffer	*What We Have Lost,* **New York Times Magazine**, October 20, 1974, p. 110.
John A. Howard	*The Proper Role of Moral Values In A Philosophy Of Education,* **Vital Speeches**, August 1, 1974, p. 665.
	There Is a Difference Between Right and Wrong, **Vital Speeches**, February 15, 1974, p. 282.
William E. Johnson, Jr.	*Lincoln and Watergate: The American Past Speaks to the American Future,* **Christian' Century**, June 25, 1975, p. 629.
Jerome Kagan	*The Dissolution of Basic Values,* **Vital Speeches**, July 15, 1973, p. 603.
Martin E. Marty	*The Values We Hold and The Values We Are,* **PTA Magazine**, June 1972, p. 6.
Bill Moyers	*The Enemy Within,* **Newsweek**, June 16, 1975, p. 84.
Senior Scholastic	*What's Right and What's Wrong With America Now?* September 15, 1969, p. 6.
E. Sloane	*The Spirits of 1776 and 1976,* **Reader's Digest**, September 1973, p. 61.
Kenneth W. Thompson	*Right and Wrong: A Framework for Moral Reasoning,* **Christian Century**, August 6-13, 1975, p. 705.
U.S. News And World Report	*Good Things About America,* April 1, 1974, p. 32.
	Who Runs America? April 21, 1975, p. 28.
Daniel Yankelovich	*A Crisis of Moral Legitimacy?* **Dissent**, Fall 1974, p. 526.

BUSINESS VALUES

Business Week	*After Watergate: Putting Business Ethics in Perspective,* September 15, 1973, p. 178.
Ronald Reagen	*Free Enterprise,* **Vital Speeches**, January 15, 1973, p. 196.
J. J. Riccardo	*American Businessman,* **Vital Speeches**, May 1, 1971, p. 434.

J. M. Roche	*Competitive System: To Work, To Preserve, To Protect,* **Vital Speeches**, May 1, 1971, p. 445.
Charles H. Smith	*Individual Freedom and Liberty: Competition and The Market Place,* **Vital Speeches**, June 1, 1974, p. 511.
Mayo J. Thompson	*Morality and Free-Enterprise,* **Vital Speeches**, January 15, 1974, p. 202.
U.S. News and World Report	*Bankruptcy — No Longer a Dirty Word,* April 7, 1975, p. 52.
	Watergate May Turn Out to Be a Catharsis to American Business, August 26, 1974, p. 67.

POLITICAL VALUES

Kenneth J Arrow	*Taxation and Democratic Values,* **New Republic**, November 2, 1974, p. 23.
Center Magazine	*Political Ethics — Then and Now,* July/August 1975, p. 63. (An interview with William Lee Miller)
Christian Century	*Another Way to Relate Religion to Politics,* November 20, 1974, p. 1083.
Commonweal	*Corruption, Conscience & Government,* March 28, 1975, p. 6.
Bruce Douglass	*Watergate and Political Realism,* **Christian Century**, October 9, 1974, p. 929.
Howard Flieger	*Morality and Politics,* **U.S. News and World Report**, November 4, 1974, p. 84.
Max Gordon	*Reclaiming the American Idea,* **Nation**, April 5, 1975, p. 409.
Sidney Lens	*For a Revolution-in-Stages,* **Progressive**, April 1974, p. 37.
	The Moral Roots of the New Despair, **Christian Century**, February 26, 1975, p. 192.
	Socialism for the Rich, **Progressive**, September 1975, p. 13.
Seymour M. Lipset and Earl Raab	*The Vacillation of the President,* **Psychology Today**, November 1973, p. 77.
Clarence E. Manion	*To the Republic: Where Is It?* **Vital Speeches**, July 15, 1974, p. 596.
Marcus Raskin	*The System Impeached,* **Progressive**, September 1974, p. 15.

Jeremy Rifkin	*George III, Inc.,* **Progressive**, July 1974, p. 28.
William E. Simon	*Getting Government Out of the Marketplace,* **Saturday Review**, July 12, 1975, p. 10.
Charles H. Smith, Jr.	*Individual Freedom and Liberty,* **Vital Speeches**, June 1, 1974, p. 511.
Casper W. Weinberger	*On Losing Our Freedom,* **Newsweek**, August 18, 1975, p. 11.

SOCIAL VALUES

The Annals	*The Changing American People: Are We Deteriorating or Improving?* July 1968 (entire issue is on this topic).
Eugene C. Bianchi	*The Superbowl Culture of Male Violence,* **Christian Century**, September 18, 1974, p. 842.
Richard A. Blake	*Movies and Myths of America,* **America**, August 16, 1975, p. 70.
Malcholm Boyd	*Journey Across America: Buoyancy and Brooding,* **Christian Century**, January 30, 1974, p. 102.
Janet Chase	*Happiness Is [among other things] Having the Lion's Share,* **Human Behavior**, July 1974, p. 56.
Christian Century	*Moral Outrage Over 'Godfather II',* January 22, 1975, p. 51.
	The Philosophy of Football, December 18, 1974, p. 1198.
Gordon J. Dahl	*The Emergence of a Leisure Ethic,* **Christian Century**, November 8, 1972, p. 1124.
Denis Goulet	*Needed: A Cultural Revolution in the U.S.,* **Christian Century**, September 4, 1974, p. 816.
David Gutmann	*Erik Erikson's America,* **Commentary**, September 1974, p. 60.
Peter Hall	*The Graying of America,* **Atlas**, April 1975, p. 41.
Arthur Herzog	*Faking It,* **Saturday Review**, March 1973, p. 36.
Ivan Hill	*Honesty and Freedom,* **Vital Speeches**, November 15, 1974, p. 93.

Herbert C. Kelman and Lee H. Lawrence *American Response to the Trial of Lt. William L. Calley,* **Psychology Today**, June 1972, p. 41.

Daniel H. Krichbaum *Masculinity and Racism — Breaking Out of the Illusion ,* **Christian Century**, January 10, 1975, p. 43.

Malachi Martin *The New Castle,* **Intellectual Digest**, May 1974, p. 54.

Richard J. Neuhaus *Is America Moral?* **Commonweal**, July 10, 1970, p. 41.

Michael Novak *Football for Feminists,* **Commonweal**, November 1974, p. 104.

Further Thoughts on Ethnicity, **Christian Century**, January 10, 1973, p. 40.

Robert C. Ouradnik *The Middle-Class Quest for Alternatives,* **Christian Century**, April 4, 1974, p. 366.

John P. Sisk *The Fear of Affluence,* **Commentary**, June 1974, p. 61.

Philip E. Slater *America's Changing Culture,* **Current**, June 1970, p. 15.

Cultures in Collision, **Psychology Today**, July 1970, p. 31.

M. J. Sobran, Jr. *The Sage and Serious Doctrine of Hugh Hefner,* **National Review**, February 1, 1974, p. 133.

U.S. News and World Report *Pursuit of Happiness — Elusive Goal in Affluent America,*   August 27, 1973, p. 34.

RELIGIOUS VALUES

The Annals *The Sixties: Radical Change in American Religion,* January 1970, (Entire issue on religion in American society.)

Garner Ted Armstrong *Spiritual Poverty,* **Plain Truth**, May 24, 1975, p. 14.

Robert N. Bellah *New Religious Consciousness,* **New Republic**, November 23, 1974, p. 33.

Christian Century · *Pietism and the Climate for Corporate Sin,* May 30, 1973, p. 619.

The Value System of a Faithless People, May 29, 1974, p. 579.

258

Christianity Today	*The Judgment of America,* November 8, 1974, p. 22.
Billy Graham	*A Spiritual Awakening,* **Vital Speeches**, April 15, 1974, p. 386.
Andrew M. Greeley	*Civil Religion and Ethnic Americans,* **Worldview**, February 1973, p. 21.
Fred M. Hechinger	*Whatever Became of Sin?* **Saturday Review**, September 21, 1974, p. 48.
Frederick Herzog	*Theology Post-Vietnam,* **Christian Century**, June 13, 1973, p. 677.
James Hitchcock	*Religion and American Culture — The Next Phase,* **Christian Century**, September 20, 1972, p. 917.
Peter McGrath	*Right Pew, Wrong Church,* **Nation**, May 17, 1975, p. 598.
Martin E. Marty	*A Nation of Behavers,* **Worldview**, May 1974, p. 9.
Gerhart Niemeyer	*What Happened to Morality?* **National Review**, November 23, 1973, p. 1300.

PATRIOTISM

Peter L. Berger	*Reflections on Patriotism,* **Worldview**, July 1974, p. 19.
William Buckley, Jr.	*The Decline of Patriotism,* **National Review**, November 10, 1972, p. 1266.
Christianity Today	*Christian As Patriot,* June 22, 1973, p. 22.
John Cogley	*Thoughts on Patriotism,* **Center Magazine**, May/June 1974, p. 2.
C. F. Henry	*Has Patriotism Had Its Day?* **Christianity Today**, June 7, 1974, p. 26.
John A. Howard	*Patriotism Revisited,* **Vital Speeches**, October 15, 1969, p. 24.
Time	*Oh, Say Can You Still See?* January 29, 1973, p. 24.

APPENDIX B
ORGANIZATIONS
TO CONTACT

The following is a partial list of organizations to contact for additional viewpoints on American values. The list is composed primarily of organizations dedicated to political and patriotic goals. For the names and addresses of organizations who comment on religious, social and economic values, consult **The Encyclopedia of Associations** at your nearest library.

The American Assembly
Columbia University
New York, N.Y. 10027

American Civil Liberties Union
22 East 40th St.
New York, N.Y. 10016

American Coalition of Patriotic Societies
15 East 90th St.
New York, N.Y. 10028

American Conservative Union
422 First St., S.E.
Capitol Hill
Washington, D.C. 20003

American Enterprise Institute
1150 Seventeenth St., N.W.
Washington, D.C. 20036

American Viewpoint, Inc.
University Square
Chapel Hill, N.C. 27514

Americanism Educational League
Freedom Center
Knott's Berry Farm
Buena Park, CA 90620

America's Manifest Destiny
2922 164th St.
Flushing, N.Y. 11358

Chamber of Commerce of the U.S.
1615 H St., N.W.
Washington, D.C. 20006

Coalition for a Democratic Majority
1823 Jefferson Place, N.W.
Washington, D.C. 20036

Committee for Economic Development
477 Madison Ave.
New York, N.Y. 10022

Common Cause
2030 M St., N.W.
Washington, D.C. 20036

Foundation for Economic Education
Irvington-on-Hudson, N.Y. 10533

Friends of Freedom
144 Darden Dr.
Waco, Texas 76706

John Birch Society
Belmont, MA 02178

Liberation Party
550 Kearny St.
San Francisco, CA 94108

Liberty Lobby
300 Independence Ave., S.E.
Washington, D.C. 20003

Moral Re-Armament, Inc.
124 East 40th St., Suite 701
New York, N.Y. 10016

Patriotic Education, Inc.
111 West Rich Ave.
P.O. Box 1088
DeLand, FL 32720

People's Bicentennial Commission
1346 Connecticut Ave., N.W.
Washington, D.C. 20036

People's Party
1404 M St., N.W.
Thomas Circle
Washington, D.C. 20005

Progressive Labor Party
G.P.O. Box 808
Brooklyn, N.Y. 11201

Republican National Committee
Dwight D. Eisenhower
Republican Center
310 First St., S.E.
Washington, D.C. 20003

The Ripon Society
1609 Connecticut Ave., N.W.
Washington, D.C. 20009

Social Democrats, U.S.A.
12th Floor / 112 East 19th St.
New York, N.Y. 10003

Socialist Workers Party
14 Charles Lane
New York, N.Y. 10014

The Twentieth Century Fund
41 East 70th St.
New York, N.Y. 10021

We the People
2422 E. Indian School Rd.
Phoenix, Arizona 85016

Young Americans for Freedom
Woodland Rd.
Sterling, VA 22170

Young Socialist Alliance
Box 471 Cooper Station
New York, N.Y. 10003

meet
the editor

DAVID L. BENDER is a history graduate from the University of Minnesota. He also has an M.A. in government from St. Mary's University in San Antonio, Texas. He has taught social problems at the high school level and is currently working on additional volumes for the Opposing Viewpoints Series.